DATE DUE

"This book offers wisdom and advice that is applicable to everyone who endeavors for a successful career and honest, genuine relationships with coworkers. I can think of at least ten people to whom I plan to give this book, beginning with both my daughters, who are preparing to enter the workforce."

—KELLY B. BROWNING, *Executive Vice President, American Institute for Cancer Research*

"An inspiring and entertaining roadmap on how to succeed in business . . . and in life. *The C Student's Guide to Success* is an excellent primer for anyone aspiring to a career in business. Ron Bliwas writes with deep insight and empathy for the majority of aspirants who don't have the advantages of birth and connections, who have to make it on their own through hard work, creativity, imagination, and a little bit of luck. Bliwas's readable and personal tale lays out the principles of success from which all of us can benefit."

—MICHAEL ALTER, *President and CEO, Alter Group*

"*The C Student's Guide to Success* is a must-read regardless of your career stage. Ron Bliwas provides practical anecdotes and solid advice that can be applied to any business. We are all C students in some areas of our personal and professional relationships and business competencies."

—STEVE LACY, *President and CEO, Meredith Corporation*

"If you weren't number one in your class or placed on the fast track in your first job, this book is for you. You'll find tips on how to catch up and overtake, and insights on marketing yourself, that you won't find anywhere else."

—SIR MARTIN SORRELL, *CEO, WPP Group*

"This book is as brash, blunt, and practical as its author. It makes great reading for all students . . . whether you got A's or C's; whether you got them last month or two decades ago, I believe you will find the insights in this book refreshing and valuable."

—SHELLY LAZARUS, *CEO, Ogilvy & Mather*

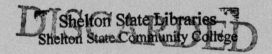
THE C STUDENT'S GUIDE TO SUCCESS

How to Become a High Achiever

Without the Best Grades, Connections, or Pedigree

RON BLIWAS

JEREMY P. TARCHER/PENGUIN
a member of Penguin Group (USA) Inc.
NEW YORK

JEREMY P. TARCHER/PENGUIN
Published by the Penguin Group
Penguin Group (USA) Inc., 375 Hudson Street, New York, New York 10014, USA •
Penguin Group (Canada), 90 Eglinton Avenue East, Suite 700, Toronto, Ontario
M4P 2Y3, Canada (a division of Pearson Penguin Canada Inc.) • Penguin Books Ltd, 80 Strand,
London WC2R 0RL, England • Penguin Ireland, 25 St Stephen's Green, Dublin 2, Ireland
(a division of Penguin Books Ltd) • Penguin Group (Australia), 250 Camberwell Road,
Camberwell, Victoria 3124, Australia (a division of Pearson Australia Group Pty Ltd) • Penguin
Books India Pvt Ltd, 11 Community Centre, Panchsheel Park, New Delhi–110 017, India •
Penguin Group (NZ), 67 Apollo Drive, Mairangi Bay, Auckland 1311, New Zealand (a division
of Pearson New Zealand Ltd) • Penguin Books (South Africa) (Pty) Ltd, 24 Sturdee Avenue,
Rosebank, Johannesburg 2196, South Africa

Penguin Books Ltd, Registered Offices: 80 Strand, London WC2R 0RL, England

Most Tarcher/Penguin books are available at special quantity discounts for bulk purchase for
sales promotions, premiums, fund-raising, and educational needs. Special books or book
excerpts also can be created to fit specific needs. For details, write Penguin Group (USA) Inc.
Special Markets, 375 Hudson Street, New York, NY 10014.

Library of Congress Cataloging-in-Publication Data

Bliwas, Ron, date.
The C student's guide to success : how to become a high achiever without the best grades,
connections, or pedigree / Ron Bliwas.
p.   cm.
ISBN 978-1-58542-556-3
1. Vocational guidance—United States.   2. College graduates—employment—United States.
3. College graduates—United States—Life skills guides.   4. School-to-work transition—United
States.   I. Title.
HF5382.5.U5B573   2007   2007000827
650.1—dc22

Printed in the United States of America
1   3   5   7   9   10   8   6   4   2

Book design by Gretchen Achilles

This publication is designed to provide accurate and authoritative information in regard to the
subject matter covered. It is sold with the understanding that the publisher is not engaged in ren-
dering legal, accounting, or other professional services. If you require legal advice or other expert
assistance, you should seek the services of a competent professional.

While the author has made every effort to provide accurate telephone numbers and Internet ad-
dresses at the time of publication, neither the publisher nor the author assumes any responsibility for errors, or for changes that occur after publication. Further, the publisher does not have any
control over and does not assume any responsibility for author or third-party websites or their
content.

To my wife, Linda, who has provided me with the support, confidence, and love every C student needs to be successful; this book, let alone my career, would not have been possible without you.

CONTENTS

INTRODUCTION

Some people are immediately coveted by employers after they graduate from college. They are the best and the brightest, students from top schools with great grades. Many of them know exactly what they want to do with their lives, and they have professors, family friends, and other well-connected people helping them achieve their goals. Right after graduating these rising stars find terrific positions with top corporations, and they never have a moment of doubt as they follow a prescribed career path.

I'm not writing this book for these people.

Instead, I'm writing for those of you who took the first job you could get and were grateful to get it. Or for those of you who took that first job, worked hard, and one day woke up and realized you were stuck in a job that was just okay. This book is also for you if you're still in school, approaching graduation, and wondering who in the world will hire you. And it's for you if you've had a few false starts or failures and want to get on the right track.

In other words, I'm writing for people like me. Though I am now an advertising agency CEO, I was an average student from the University of Arizona who grew up in Coraopolis, Pennsylvania. I could have used a book like this. It would have helped me to understand how to use my natural talents—my storytelling ability, my relationship-building skills—to compete with those who were more academically accomplished or more polished than I was.

Career opportunities and strategies are different for people like you and me than for Harvard MBAs. When you're not viewed as the best of the best or lack a clear career path, you need an alternative approach. This book will provide one.

Let me explain how by telling you a bit about myself and how I came to write this book.

WORKING AT THE WRONG COMPANY IN THE WRONG POSITION FOR ALMOST NO MONEY

At first the job offer from H.J. Heinz in Pittsburgh seemed like a great opportunity. I was about to be married and needed to find a job, and the chance to start out in Heinz's training program sounded perfect. It was the first job offer I received, and I took it without a second thought.

I immediately was assigned to Heinz's baby food division, and my job consisted of traveling from store to store in Pennsylvania, opening up cases of Heinz baby food, and putting the jars on the shelves. Of course I didn't know beforehand that this was what I would be doing. On my first day of work I arrived in the supermarket parking lot in my brand-new suit. I looked and felt terrific, every inch the business executive on his way to the top. My supervisor met me and escorted me first into the supermarket and then the storeroom in back where boxes of baby food were piled to the ceiling. He told me to climb up and start handing them down. "You want me to do that?" I asked. The supervisor shook his head and gave me a look that let me know who I was: a naive twenty-one-year-old from the University of Arizona. I spent the morning handing down boxes and turning my beautiful suit into a dusty, dirty mess.

As demeaning and demoralizing as the work was, though, I would have stuck with it if I had been in the right place for someone like me. It soon became clear that I would never have a chance to succeed at H.J. Heinz.

One of my regular customers at Heinz was the largest volume grocery store in Pittsburgh. They also had one of the largest baby food sections of any store in the country, using this category as a loss leader (a strategy where products may lose money but achieve others' marketing goals). The two men who owned the store did not have children to pass it on to, and they essentially adopted me. I always struck up a conversation with them when I visited their store. Though I was twenty-one and they must have been in their early sixties, I naturally found common ground with them and pretty soon my visits entailed going to their office, having coffee, and talking. They seemed to enjoy hearing about my life, and one day they made me a job offer.

I was honest with them. I explained that I hated the grocery business. Amazingly, they didn't mind that I had turned them down. In fact, they said they wanted to help me: "What can we do for you?" they asked. I suggested that they eliminate Heinz's two competitors, Beech-Nut and Gerber, from their shelves and make it an all-Heinz department.

"Done," they said.

This was a coup, especially for someone as young and inexperienced as I was. I had managed to create the largest all-Heinz baby food department in the world. The president of Heinz visited the store and the publicity department took his picture next to the display. It was the sort of thing that could make a career.

It didn't make mine. I received no bonus or recognition of any kind. I should have seen the writing on the wall. I was not viewed as executive material when I was hired, and I would never be viewed that way.

After six months at Heinz I was truly miserable. I sensed I had something to contribute but didn't know what. So I decided to take my one week of vacation and go to Chicago to look for an ad agency job. Though I was not a particularly attractive candidate, I was astute enough to realize I had one thing going for me: I knew the grocery business. Or at the very least, I knew the business better than the other candidates applying for entry-level account positions. For this reason I focused my search on agencies with food accounts. Edward H. Weiss & Company was a midsize agency whose clients included Thomas J. Lipton Co. (makers of Wish-Bone salad dressing), and they were looking for an assistant account executive. During the interview I told them I might not know much about the agency business, but I knew exactly what went on in grocery stores and that their food clients might value that knowledge.

They agreed, and hired me. At the same time, they also hired a recent Northwestern University MBA named Mike. Without a doubt, Mike had a better pedigree than I did. I'm sure his SAT scores would have put mine to shame. He also was well-versed in the details of the job. One of my responsibilities was to calculate per capita consumption, market share, and other research relevant to our clients, and Mike was kind enough to give me the formulas for doing so—I had them laminated and placed them in my wallet, knowing that, unlike Mike, I could not do these calculations in my head. On paper, Mike was eminently more qualified for the job than I was. In the office, though, it was no contest. Mike was introverted and spent much of his time in the cubicle. I was gregarious and knew everyone in the agency within a short period of time.

Because of my visibility, the head of client services called me into his office when the agency was fired by one of their clients,

WBBM-TV, a CBS affiliate. This client, furious at the poor quality of service it was receiving, told the agency they no longer wanted to see the guy who was handling the account. Still, until the client-agency relationship was officially dissolved, a significant amount of detail work remained. The client services head, aware that I was personable and eager, decided to make me the sacrificial lamb.

The client contact was Bruce Bloom, who stood six feet, six inches tall. When I walked into Bruce's office for the first time and identified myself, he began screaming at me, accusing the agency of being incompetent and stupid, lacing his diatribe with language more befitting a locker room than a place of business. As an ex-jock, though, I had been in lots of locker rooms. I didn't run out of his office in terror or start screaming back at him.

Instead, I held up a hand like a traffic cop and said, "Hey, I haven't done anything wrong yet. If I do something wrong, then scream. Until then, don't. I'll do the best job I can, and if I do something wrong, tell me and I'll try to do it better."

He calmed down. More than that, he eventually warmed up to me. After I worked with him for a few weeks, we went out for coffee. After a few months, my wife and I start seeing Bruce and his wife socially. Then one day the agency CFO called me into his office and told me I needed to talk with Bruce about their search for another agency and when they would officially fire us; he was in the process of doing his next-year budgeting and wanted to factor this information into his calculations.

I went over to the television station and told Bruce I needed to talk to him.

"You look so serious," he said, ushering me into his office.

"This is a serious conversation."

I told him about my discussion with the CFO and asked him if they were close to choosing another agency.

"What are you talking about?"

"You fired us," I said.

"Yeah, but that was before you. We think you're great. You're our agency."

I returned to the office with the good news, but aside from some halfhearted congratulations, I received nothing substantive in return for my efforts. What I did receive, though, was another valuable lesson about career success. I was coming to realize that in some organizations, no matter what you do, you can't succeed unless you're a certain type of individual. I was also learning that good relationships produce good results.

This was the start of the learning process that forms the core of this book.

THE COMBINED WISDOM OF OVERACHIEVERS, UNLIKELY VISIONARIES AND STREET-SMART ENTREPRENEURS

Though my own experiences were the inspiration for this book, they were just the starting point. I have interviewed a wide range of highly successful people, some close friends and others I had never met until the interview session. On the surface, these individuals may seem to have nothing in common. Flip Filipowski is a risk-taking, high-tech entrepreneur whose tenure as head of Divine was marked by both innovation and well-publicized controversy. Sam Morasca was a Shell Oil marketing executive for many years, and his personality and career path are the opposite of Flip's. Louise O'Sullivan is a former schoolteacher who became the CEO of a midsize engineering-based company; she succeeded as a woman in a male-dominated industry and as a nonengineer in a company dominated by engineers.

What unites all these high achievers, though, is that they overcame significant obstacles in order to succeed. Some had undistinguished academic records. Others were "characters," true originals who possessed what people used to refer to as moxie but lacked a buttoned-down business demeanor. Still others experienced false starts and failures and were counted out by those who didn't know them well.

None of them would have overcome these obstacles if they had followed the conventional career wisdom: trying to secure jobs at the largest companies in their fields, never taking a new job unless it offered more money and a higher-level position, focusing exclusively on obtaining knowledge and skills required for a promotion. Each succeeded by adopting remarkably similar attitudes and actions. I was amazed at how their success factors resembled my own. Most of their stories revealed how their ability to be keen observers and professional learners enabled them to take advantage of opportunities. Many of them talked about how hard they labored to be compassionate, honest human beings, and how they were rewarded for these qualities. A number of them discussed how far trusting their instincts had taken them. These commonalities eventually coalesced into the traits that define each chapter, as well as the final piece of advice that is the theme of the final chapter.

These individuals also provided me with wonderful stories— instructive, inspiring, and sometimes laugh-out-loud funny—that you'll find throughout the book. I should tell you up front that I am a storyteller and a lover of other people's stories. I've found that people pay attention to stories in a way they don't pay attention to lectures. Through the humor, emotion, or drama of an anecdote, you can deliver a message with a wallop . . . and without being boring or pedantic.

Speaking of boring, that's one trait none of the interviewees share. Rich Melman, for instance, is the founder and head of Lettuce Entertain You Enterprises. Rich is probably the country's most successful restaurateur, and I was mesmerized as I listened to him talk about opening his first restaurant and his growing anxiety as days turned into weeks and still no one showed up. He told me about his absolute terror of embarrassing himself, and how it drove him to work incredibly hard and creatively in order to avoid that outcome. As I listened to him, I realized that many of the individuals I talked to were driven by a similar fear—as was I.

Most of the people I interviewed have allowed me to use their names, but a handful of them asked me to disguise their identities. In some instances, I simply used a pseudonym, and in other cases I created a composite character. You'll know I'm using a pseudonym or composite when only a first name is given. You'll also find brief biographies of all high achievers who granted me permission to use their names at the end of this book.

I should also point out that not all the people you'll read about were C students. Though I and a number of others were not stellar students and did not attend the most selective of colleges, some of these high achievers were excellent students—one even went to Harvard! The C student in this book's title is meant to be metaphorical. All of us entered our careers with disadvantages. We weren't voted most likely to succeed. Most of us had some kind of career handicap, be it grades, gender, social circumstances, financial problems, or false starts.

Finally, even the worst students among us succeeded because of street smarts, emotional intelligence, or some other form of brainpower not measured by SAT scores. As you'll see, these individuals are off-the-charts smart when it comes to producing results.

HOW TO GET THE MOST OUT OF THIS BOOK

This isn't a textbook, and I'm not going to give you a formula for being successful. While I hope the nine career suggestions that make up the book's first nine chapters will help your career, I don't expect you to follow them as if they were the nine commandments. Because of your personality or your circumstances, some of the suggestions may be difficult for you to use. It may be that just one or two pieces of advice are all you need to kick your career into high gear. You may discover that "relying on many mentors" is what catalyzes your career. Someone else may begin "selling what he believes," and as soon as he stops being cynical and starts being honest with his ideas, he receives the promotions that were so elusive before. One of the suggestions is "trust your instincts," and I advise you to trust your gut as to what you can take from these pages and apply to your own life.

The advice you'll encounter is different from what you'll find in most career books. I'm not going to tell you how to interview for a job or put together a résumé. I'm not going to offer advice about how to get a job at the world's most prestigious consulting firm or for the country's largest company because, frankly, those aren't the types of jobs C students usually get. Instead, I'm going to share stories that inspire, entertain, and instruct and offer some ideas about how to put the lessons of the stories to work in your career.

For example, in the chapter on mentors (and in other chapters as well) you'll encounter Alvin Eicoff, the man who hired me and was the founder of the agency I head today. Many books will tell you how to find a mentor, and I guarantee none of their advice would point you in the direction of someone like Al. From his example I learned that mentors don't have to be perfect; they don't have to fulfill your ideal of success. If he were still alive and I could bring him into the room where you are now and introduce him, you might think he was a car salesman or the owner of a store that sells loud, garish clothing. You might admire his enormous energy and passion, but you might also find him to be loud and intolerant. One second he would be revealing a brilliant insight about the psychology behind television advertising, and the next he would be telling you an off-color joke. If you didn't know who Al was and I told you he was the father of television direct-response advertising, named by *Advertising Age* as one of television's pioneers, and in the Direct Marketing Association Hall of Fame, you would never believe me.

I learned something from Al almost every day, and often it was an unexpected lesson. Once Al and I were going to see a client, and it promised to be a difficult meeting. Our commercial for their product, a stain remover, had failed miserably. On the way there I asked Al what he was going to tell the client, and he shrugged and said he didn't know. We arrived, and the meeting got off to a terrible start. The client attacked us for failing to move enough product, lambasting our strategy.

"You're in the wrong business," Al suddenly said.

That got everyone's attention. They all watched him and wondered what he meant. After a dramatic pause, he continued, "You should be in the guitar business."

What Al said made no sense. But it also was exactly the right thing to say. It defused the tension in the room and allowed us to move on to other matters. More than that, though, it helped me understand why Al was so successful. His ego would not allow him to admit failure. He simply couldn't say what just about everyone else would have said: "We made a mistake."

I'm not suggesting that the key to success is never admitting you're wrong. Al inspired confidence in others because of his enormous ego. As insecure as he was deep inside, he only showed people his conviction that he was right. You wanted him to be your advertising guy because he seemed like a force of nature. You figured that one way or another he would find a way to make your advertising work. And most of the time you'd be right.

I knew Al was the right mentor, in part because he needed me as much as I needed him. For all of Al's strengths, he wasn't polished or a good manager; he had reached the point where he required a partner to help bring in the larger corporate clients, who sometimes couldn't get past his unpolished demeanor. Finding a mentor, therefore, isn't just a one-way street. As you'll discover in the chapter on this topic, it's as much about what you can do for the mentor as what he can do for you.

SUCCESS DEPENDS ON WHO YOU ARE, NOT WHERE YOU CAME FROM

A recent study revealed that twenty years after graduating college, students who attended Ivy League schools had roughly the same income as students who graduated from "lesser" colleges. As surprising at this might seem on the surface, it confirms what I have observed. Over the years, I have seen a pattern in which the people who get the top jobs—who become CEOs, entrepreneurial successes, top lawyers, high-tech gurus—are often those from humble academic, social, and financial beginnings. I have also observed that the people who are deemed most likely to succeed often don't, at least not to the extent that everyone had expected. A number of years ago, I had an employee who was academically brilliant—Karl probably never received less than an A in his life. He never had a problem getting a job because he projected an aura of confidence and intelligence. Karl certainly was competent, but he never excelled. My theory was that his extraordinary intelligence made him lazy; things always came too easily for him. He was never driven to prove himself or to compete. He also had an arrogance about him that was off-putting, preventing him from building the range of relationships critical for success in the advertising business.

Many of you may doubt yourself for any number of reasons. Maybe you weren't a good student, you went to an average school, you lack connections, you were fired from or quit your first few jobs, or you don't seem to possess the polished style your colleagues exhibit. I am here to tell you that none of this matters.

I realize that we live in a society that esteems academic achievement and where people remember their SAT scores long after they've forgotten the name of their high school sweethearts. Still, let me leave you with a story that I hope will help you to see that you have as much of a chance of being successful as anyone.

A while back I attended a Young Presidents' Organization (YPO) event and was seated next to the dean of the University of Chicago Business School. I asked him if his school offered a course in salesmanship, and he said no.

"Why not?" I asked.

He shrugged and said, as if the answer were obvious, "We're the University of Chicago."

I insisted to him that most of his students would fail to reach their potential unless they knew how to sell, and he suggested I address this subject in a talk.

I gave a speech at the U of C titled "How to Make It in the Real World" and emphasized to the students that if they could not sell themselves and their ideas, they would have trouble being as successful as they wanted to be. I asked the hundreds of students in the auditorium to raise their hands if they had ever sold anything in their lives. Three people raised their hands. When I told them that without the ability to sell, the most they could hope for was a job in middle management, they looked at me like I was nuts. They had always gotten by on their brains.

When I returned home that evening and told my family about the experience, my twelve-year-old son, Michael, asked me if the

University of Chicago was a good school. I told him it was one of the five best schools in the country.

"How come you didn't go there?" he asked.

"I wasn't smart enough."

"That doesn't make sense," Michael said. "How can you be smart enough to talk to them and teach them but you weren't smart enough to go there?"

I didn't have an answer for him then, but I have an answer for you now: There are all types of smarts, and this book will help you make the most of the type you have.

CHAPTER 1

MAKE THE MOST OUT OF
MANY MENTORS

I have had four mentors. One you met in the introductory chapter, a man who was as brilliant as he was eccentric. Another mentor was the most famous individual in the history of advertising. A third was the chairman of a large ad agency, whose competitive nature made him highly successful but also almost cost me my life. A fourth taught me a valuable lesson by refusing to tell me what I was doing wrong.

Four mentors may seem like a lot, but C students can use all the help they can get. A number of people profiled in these pages had unusual or unlikely mentors, and sometimes more than a few. Being open-minded about who you can learn from is an important skill to master. If you turn away from someone because he doesn't fit your idea of who a mentor should be, you're going to miss out. Likewise, certain individuals may look like mentors but in reality they're anything but.

Some people are the wrong mentors for you or anyone else; they may occupy leadership positions, but they are bullies or egomaniacs or possess other traits that will do you more harm than good. Others may be good mentors for Harvard MBAs but aren't particularly good teachers, a quality you should prize above all others. I'll help you determine which ones are likely to help you the most.

You may also go after a mentor in the wrong way. The best and the brightest usually attract senior people who want to help rising stars, but you may not automatically find yourself being mentored. You're going to have to be proactive, but that doesn't mean being overly aggressive and scaring people off. I'll share some dos and don'ts about how to establish and strengthen a relationship with a mentor.

Finally, I'll tell you some stories about mentors who greatly helped my career and the careers of others.

Let's start out, though, by focusing on the process of finding someone who can teach you some things you'll never learn in school.

THE SEARCH FOR THE PERSON WHO POSSESSES THE WISDOM

Sam Morasca, who became the top marketing person at Shell Oil, offers great advice about finding a mentor: "Get into a high-profile position, so when you perform, you get noticed." Sam instinctively recognized that if he were to get shuttled into a job where he was slogging along with everyone else, he would be overlooked even if he performed at a superhuman level. Other people came into big corporations with far more impressive pedigrees than he had, and their performance was automatically going to be in the spotlight; his would be in the shadows unless he found a job that gave him high visibility. It was for this reason that he turned down a job offer from Alcoa for more money. During the interview process, he was given a tour of Alcoa and was shown a room where fifty people were all doing the same thing. "You'll be one of them," Sam was told. He took the job at Shell because he knew he was the only one who would be assigned to a particular marketing study—a study that the company had a lot riding on—and as a result of his work, a mentor adopted him. As Sam has said, "When you're starting out and they give you a shovel, make sure people see you when you're shoveling."

I did the same thing in my first agency job. I made it my business to talk to everyone and volunteer for any project where I had a chance to shine, and I have no doubt that my first mentor took me on because I was impossible to ignore. I made it my business to visit regularly with everyone, from secretaries to the CEO. Even a blind man would have known who I was, since I was always asking for things to do. People notice volunteers faster than they notice conscripts.

A wise man once told me "You don't find mentors; mentors find you," meaning that someone with wisdom and experience is more likely to pick you out of a crowd than vice versa. This is an especially relevant point for people who aren't designated as high-potential trainees when they start their careers. You may see someone you'd like to have as a mentor, but you may not be in a position to be mentored. If a given individual is highly respected in the company and in a top position, he probably has his choice of mentees, and if you lack rising star status you may not seem like a good candidate. Increase your visibility, and you will have a major impact on whether a mentor finds you.

As eager as you may be to attract a mentor, be selective. This may sound like strange advice, since you may feel that beggars can't be choosers. You're not a beggar, though, and if you think that way it will be a self-fulfilling prophecy. Everyone has a strength, and no doubt you possess a skill or a character trait that is going to make a senior person want to lend you a hand. Maybe she will see a bit of herself in you, or your diligence and willingness to work hard will impress her. Whatever the reason, you'll find plenty of mentors out there, but some of them won't be right for you.

Screen your prospective mentors. The following criteria will help you do so:

1. LOOK FOR A MENTOR WHO WILL ALLOW YOU TO ASK FORGIVENESS RATHER THAN PERMISSION.

The above paraphrases advice from Yitzhak Azizis, an Israeli management consultant. His point is: Find a mentor who will allow you to make mistakes and does not demand that you seek his approval before you do anything. Ideally, mentors are guides. They should give you plenty of room to learn and grow, gently pointing you in the right direction when you go off course. Too many people, though, seek mentors who will give them all the answers, and there is no learning in that. As a C student, you may lack the confidence to make mistakes, so it's critical that you find a savvy executive who tolerates well-intentioned errors.

Your mentor may be your direct boss or someone higher up in the organization, but whoever it is, avoid controlling, micromanaging types. They will make it impossible for you to take risks and learn from your mistakes, and this is something every C student needs to experience.

2. LOOK FOR A MENTOR YOU CAN TRUST.

People who aren't immediately dubbed high potentials can be susceptible to bad mentors. If you're needy, you may attach yourself to someone who treats you like a lackey because you feel you deserve that type of role. Most companies have senior people who are game players and manipulators, who are cynical, pessimistic, and even immoral. Unfortunately, they may also be charming. I know of one executive with a large corporation who adopted specific types of rookies—people from middle-of-the-road MBA programs who seemed a bit intimidated or insecure. This executive took these rookies under his wing, but he did so without any desire to help them make a successful transition to corporate life. Instead, he was just looking for lackeys who would do the work he didn't want to do himself. He treated his direct reports in the same way as he did his mentees, every so often offering them a bit of advice in exchange for them doing a lot of tasks he wasn't interested in doing.

Even worse, though, is a mentor who models unethical behavior. On the surface she may seem charming and even charismatic, but underneath she is a schemer and charlatan. She may teach a mentee that the way to get ahead is to manipulate and cheat, or that the only thing that matters is results, and it doesn't matter how you get them. C students are especially vulnerable to unethical mentors because they may think that they need an edge to get ahead, and that this mentor will give them that edge. Unethical and amoral types don't get far, more so today than ever before. In most companies values are important, and individuals who don't share these values are seen as flawed. They may be highly competent at what they do, but they aren't viewed as real leaders.

To find a leader you can trust, don't just rely on what you see; ask other people what they think of a possible mentor. Ask questions that give you a sense of her values: Is she honest? If someone tells her something in confidence, does she honor that confidence? Is she willing to go to bat for people if she believes in them?

3. LOOK FOR A MENTOR YOU ENJOY SPENDING TIME WITH.

Whether a mentor is your direct boss or someone else in the organization, you may end up spending a great deal of time with him. So think about whether you like a prospective mentor and enjoy being with him. A mentor doesn't have to be your best friend or even someone you socialize with, but ideally you'll look forward to seeing him, which increases the odds that you'll seek him out when you need help. This doesn't mean your mentor should be just like you. Al Eicoff, for instance, was my opposite in many ways, but I loved talking with him. He was a larger-than-life character, and he always had something provocative to say. He made me laugh and he made me think, so I was always eager to go into his office and hear what he had to say.

Which senior people in your company do you enjoy talking to? Is there someone you're especially eager to see, whom you naturally turn to when you have a question? Avoid individuals who make you feel uncomfortable, people you find boring or pedantic.

4. LOOK FOR A MENTOR WHO HAS SOMETHING TO TEACH THAT YOU NEED TO LEARN.

This piece of advice may seem obvious, but it's not one that a lot of people put into practice. For instance, you may find a mentor who has something to teach you, but it's not something you *need* to learn; it's something of secondary importance. Recognize the knowledge and skills you must acquire to do well in your chosen profession, and keep an eye out for bosses who might be able to help you acquire the requisite information and competencies. Early in my career I had a mentor, Bob Immen, who was a solid writer. I realized that I would have to become competent at writing everything from letters to reports, and that Bob could teach me to become a decent writer. The way he taught me, though, was a bit unusual. For example, one day he had me write a report for him. After he read it, he handed it back and said, "Do it again." So

I rewrote the report, and Bob handed it back without any suggestions, simply repeating, "Do it again." Over and over I rewrote it, discovering more mistakes each time. Bob allowed me to discover what was wrong with the writing on my own, and this painstaking process taught me to think before I wrote. Finally, when I handed in the report and he accepted it, I had a great sense of accomplishment. More than that, I had been taught a valuable lesson from a mentor.

I should also emphasize that different people are going to teach you different things. You may have a boss who is not your mentor, but he does a decent job of teaching you the basics and helping you become competent at your work. A mentor, though, teaches you a lot more. There's a phrase that captures what a mentor can give you: "learning the ropes." Originally a nautical term, it meant that new sailors had to learn which rope hauled up which sail. A mentor should give you the same sort of essential advice. What do you really need to understand to be successful at your current job, to be promoted to higher-level jobs and in your career?

Beyond these suggestions, you should also approach a prospective mentor slowly and with knowledge. Becky Jewett, who has been CEO of a number of direct-marketing companies, says, "It's a real turnoff when a distant acquaintance announces, 'I want you to mentor me.'" Instead, she prefers that a person take on additional responsibilities first, and shine, making her want to mentor him. Another way of looking at Becky's advice is that you should first establish a relationship with a potential mentor before moving that relationship to a mentoring level. This will give both of you a chance to see if it's a good match.

The best way to approach mentors with knowledge is to try to find some common ground. Many people who lack experience or confidence think that a top person in their organization wouldn't be interested in them. They're right . . . unless they can gather information that enables them to make a connection. Perhaps this prospective mentor played football in college, and you did, too. Perhaps her spouse and your spouse grew up in the same town. Maybe you are both passionate about jazz. A lot is usually known about organizational leaders. If you ask any veteran employee something about a CEO or vice president, the odds are they'll know the answers. In most instances, you'll find a common interest or experience that you can use to make a connection with this person. It doesn't guarantee that she'll become your mentor, but it does give you a way to make an impression and create a small bond.

BE OPEN TO A WIDE RANGE OF MENTORS

I suggest you think of mentors in the broadest terms possible. The classic definition of a mentor is very limiting, especially for C students. If you target one individual whom you expect to mentor you for the next twenty years, you'll miss out on a lot of learning. Odds are, you probably have some gaps in your education or you're going to need help in more areas than any one person can help you with. It is not a level playing field. The person in the office next door to you may have considerable advantages in terms of his education, his pull within the company, and his network of contacts. He may have done an internship that gave him experiences you don't yet have. You may have an unwritten black mark next to your name because you took five years off searching for your true profession or because you're not as socially polished as the next guy. Different mentors can do a good job of helping you make up lost ground. One might teach you how to be a better communicator while another might model a leadership style that you can adopt and adapt.

To help you understand why it's important to be open to different types of mentors, let me share a few stories with you.

Former Illinois state senator Howie Carroll recognized at age thirteen that Chicago mayor Richard J. Daley could be his mentor. He may not have consciously thought this to himself, but he recognized that the mayor had all the qualities I enumerated in the introduction. The mayor immediately took to Howie when he was young, and Howie immediately saw that the mayor had skills and wisdom that could help him, regardless of what career he ultimately chose.

Other people might have decided that the mayor of a large city—especially someone as powerful and as intimidating as Mayor Daley—would not be a suitable mentor. The typical C student might ask himself, "Why would someone like that take the time or trouble to help someone like me?" Howie, though, saw that the mayor liked his sense of humor and the fact that Howie wasn't afraid of him. One particular incident illustrates how this recognition dawned on Howie.

Howie was in eighth grade. The mayor was friends with Howie's father; Howie had met the mayor a few years before and talked to him briefly. Howie was working on a project for his civics class that related to a public works plan the mayor was going to announce. Howie asked his dad about it, and his father suggested that he call the mayor and request an interview that he could then incorporate into his class project. Howie called, and the mayor's office made an appointment for Howie to come down and see the mayor.

Howie arrived at City Hall a few hours before the mayor's five-year plan was going to be released to the public, and he was escorted past various secretaries and other sentries into the mayor's private office. They began talking, and Howie noticed the five-year plan on the desk had an "embargoed until noon" sticker on it.

"You look puzzled," the mayor said to Howie.

"What does embargo mean?"

The mayor told him but noticed that Howie still looked puzzled.

"Well," Howie said, "you were elected to a four-year term, but this is a five-year plan."

"What does that mean to you?"

Howie thought for a moment and then said, "It means you have to be elected to another term if you're going to complete the plan."

The mayor laughed and said, "You're the first one to figure it out. You've got an instinct for politics."

From that moment on, Howie and the mayor would talk regularly, and the mayor would provide him with numerous lessons and assistance that would serve him well throughout his career.

A number of people I interviewed noted that their mentors were not official mentors, but people who had tremendous influence on them when they were younger and who modeled behavior that served them well during their careers. More than one person mentioned a family member—a parent, an uncle—who had a profound influence on their success. Many times, the memory of what a relative said or did would provide guidance even long after the relative had passed away.

Art Frigo, a highly successful entrepreneur and business school professor, suggests another mentor type: "A great strategy for a C student is to be mentored by the president of a small company." By definition, the president of a small company has to do it all.

He needs to know how to sell, deal with financial issues, create strategy, and get things done. Art believes that finding someone who will essentially let you be his apprentice can provide the type of learning that would take years to acquire elsewhere.

Mentors, then, come in every imaginable shape and size, and if you limit your mentors' number or type, you limit what you can learn. Following is a list of several different types of mentors. You may want to find at least one in each category.

- LEADERSHIP MENTOR. If you aspire to move into a leadership position, you need to find someone who can model leadership behaviors. This person can teach you everything from how to delegate to how to communicate a strategy. Certainly CEOs are great mentors in this regard, but many vice presidents are strong leaders and can provide the same lessons.

- SKILLS MENTOR. This is someone who possesses one or more skills that you suspect will be critical for you. I needed to learn to write well; you may need to learn to speak well. It may also involve learning more technical skills based on job function.

- KNOWLEDGE MENTOR. What you learn from this mentor is more generalized than the specific skills the skills mentor offers. This person may know a lot about how to obtain resources or may simply be wise about the dos and don'ts of a career. Some of the best mentors are ones who can serve as sounding boards for your ideas and offer suggestions and information to help you achieve your goals.

- NON-WORK-RELATED MENTOR. This can be anyone from a family member to a famous politician, and the person can be living or dead. This is an individual you can draw inspiration from and whose life and behavior provide a good model for your own. Unlike work mentors, these individuals may not be available to answer your questions about how to obtain a promotion, but they can offer you valuable lessons about ambition and an ethical way of approaching your goals.

- PRIMARY MENTOR. This is someone with whom you interact regularly, and it can be any of the above types except the non-work-related mentor. Al Eicoff was my primary mentor. Yours may be your direct boss or someone in the organization with whom you form a particularly close bond.

- SECONDARY MENTOR. This can be an elder statesman who has great respect in the industry and whom you turn to only occasionally, or it may be a guru with particular expertise in an area in which you're interested.

There are two other points about mentor types that you should keep in mind. First, if you change companies, you will probably need a new mentor in the new company. Remember, though, that many people still rely on mentors from their previous companies to provide guidance. In fact, sometimes when your mentor is no longer your superior he can be freer with his advice and less worried about charges of favoritism. Second, more and more people are finding that veteran consultants make good mentors. You may work with a consultant on a project and find that he is brilliant, that the diversity of his experience is invaluable. He may be willing to mentor you because you are a current or potential future client, and you should certainly take advantage of the relationship if you feel this individual has a lot to offer you.

HOW TO MAXIMIZE YOUR MENTORING RELATIONSHIP

Some people take mentoring for granted. Their mentors are looking out for them and they want to help them learn and grow, but these people can be very passive—they don't ask many questions and fail to take advantage of a mentor's knowledge and experiences. At the other extreme, some people actively resist a mentor's advice, responding defensively to their suggestions.

Don't be passive or overly aggressive. Instead, maximize the relationship by taking three steps.

1. MAKE SURE THE RELATIONSHIP IS A TWO-WAY STREET.

In other words, this isn't just about you. Mentors are not always taking you under their wing out of purely altruistic motives. They may adopt you because they feel it is their responsibility to develop leadership talent. They may want a bright young person to be a sounding board for their ideas. They may see you as the right person to carry out special assignments. Whatever the reason, you need to give something back to make it a win-win relationship. Don't underestimate your ability to give back, even if you feel like you don't know anything. Your mentor probably sees things in you that you don't see in yourself.

Mayor Daley, for instance, was the most powerful mayor in the country, but he expected Howie Carroll to learn how to think for himself and to come up with solutions to problems, not just take orders. Fortunately, Howie understood this dynamic, as the following example illustrates.

During Mayor Daley's tenure, tax incremental financing became a major issue, and Howie, as a state senator, had chaired a hearing attended by representatives of three of the biggest developers in

Chicago: Phil Klutznick, Arthur Rubloff, and Harry Chaddick. They had definite views on this issue and wanted Howie's support. After the hearing, Howie went to Mayor Daley to solicit his advice. Howie walked him through the ins and outs of tax incremental financing, mentioning the three developers. The mayor discussed looking at legislation based on "who does it help and who does it hurt" and the importance of helping friends. Then he said, "You know, these three are great friends, but I haven't heard from them."

Howie immediately knew that this was not an idle comment; the mayor wanted to be asked and wanted to give these three powerful developers a gentle reprimand, but he didn't want to give an "order" to Howie. Rather, he wanted to see how Howie would deal with the lesson he was being taught. Howie made appointments with each man individually, and after a bit of preamble he suggested that it might be in their best interest if they would request an audience with their friend the mayor and ask for his support.

A week later, Howie received a summons to the mayor's office. When he walked in, he saw the mayor was beaming. Howie asked him why he was so happy.

"My friends came to see me—they were here yesterday. Remember that thing you were talking about, tax incremental financing? It turns out, my friends would like it—can you see your way clear to helping them? I wonder how they got the idea to come see me?"

The last was said with a distinct twinkle in the mayor's eye.

2. MEET YOUR MENTOR'S CHALLENGES.

Expect mentors to test you, to give you stretch assignments, or put you in positions that you find uncomfortable. As a C student, your temptation may be to say, "I can't do this." Don't give in to the temptation. If you have a good mentor, she'll be an astute judge of your capabilities. If your mentor is not your boss, she may put you on projects or give you special assignments that you otherwise never would have had a chance to work on. As intimidating as these assignments might be or as unqualified as you might feel, take them on. Even if you fail, they provide great opportunities for learning. Perhaps even more important, they demonstrate to your mentor that you're eager to learn and that you respect her judgment. These challenges may also separate you from the pack.

Bill Phillips became Ogilvy & Mather's chairman shortly after they purchased A. Eicoff & Co., and he was also my mentor, though he was a very different one from Al Eicoff. Polished and sophisticated, he taught me crucial advertising lessons about creating strategies, establishing a strong management style, and dealing with blue-chip clients. His challenges, though, weren't limited to work. We were both good athletes and fierce competitors, and we started out playing tennis together. As good a tennis player as Bill was, he could never win more than two games from me, and it drove him crazy. Still, he wasn't about to stop trying to beat me, either in tennis or in other athletic endeavors. Once when we were at a heads-of-office meeting in Switzerland, he invited me to accompany him skiing.

"We'll take the Haute Route," he said.

"What's that?"

"Oh, it requires you to climb a bit, but it gives you access to a mountain between Switzerland and Italy, and you can ski endless powder."

That sounded like fun, and since I was good skier I didn't think twice about accepting his invitation. Even when I started receiving calls from other Ogilvy executives warning me against this expedition, I didn't change my mind. They told me that Bill was absolutely nuts when it came to taking risks and that the Haute Route was grueling even for top-level skiers. None of that bothered me. I was twelve years younger than Bill and in great shape. I reassured the Ogilvy people that I could do anything he could do. I also knew that it was something I had to do. Bill was my mentor, he had given me a challenge, and to fail to take him up on it would certainly diminish me in his eyes. One of the reasons he was my mentor was our intensely competitive relationship, and so I would have been ill-advised to decline his invitation.

In hindsight, while taking the challenge made career sense, I should not have been so quick to brush aside the Ogilvy executives' warnings. The adage "Fools rush in where angels fear to tread" is applicable. We took a lift to the top of a mountain in Zermatt with a guide and Bill's three other guests, two of whom were former ski instructors. We were told to remove our skis and start hiking up the mountain to skiable terrain. It was not just steep; sheer drops of ten thousand feet and slippery conditions made the experience terrifying. At one point I slipped and started sliding down toward a crevasse. Unable to stop my downward plunge, I was certain I was going over the edge. Fortunately, the guide managed to grab my rucksack and pulled me to safety. Later that day, we encountered a cliff that we couldn't hike past, so we had to rappel seventy feet down on a rope. At that point, I was sending up prayers to God, telling Him that if he let me live I'd never put myself in danger again. One of our party fell and suffered a wound. Then a huge snowstorm came in, but we managed to make it to a hut, where we spent the night. All of Bill's guests vowed not to repeat what we did the next day. The next day dawned, though, and Bill talked us into trying it again. The conditions were even worse, and Bill finally realized he had pushed us too far. He contacted

Swiss Army guards to have them escort us down the mountain. To get down, we had to ski through seemingly vertical chutes where if you fall, you're dead. We made it back safely, and the next day, as I was talking on the phone to Ken Roman, Ogilvy's North America CEO, Bill walked into Ken's office. Ken told him he was talking to me, and Bill got on the line.

"Well, do you have any respect for me now?" the unrepentant competitor asked me.

I tell this story not to suggest that you should do everything your mentor requests, but to communicate that taking on his challenges can mean a great deal to your career. Not only did this experience cement my relationship with Bill and allow me to pick his brain, but it gave me a significant boost within Ogilvy. Bill had an aura, and some of that aura rubbed off on me. People were aware that he was mentoring me; they frequently saw us together. That was enough to open doors that had been closed and helped me build a network within the company.

3. ACCEPT YOUR MENTOR'S IMPERFECTIONS.

Some C students look up to their mentors with stars in their eyes, believing they can do no wrong. They are blinded by their inferiority complexes; they are so grateful for the help that they refuse to see the flaw that every leader has, no matter how successful he is. At some point, however, they are confronted with evidence of a mentor's imperfections that they can't ignore, and they're terribly disappointed. They are so disappointed, in fact, that they have difficulty maintaining the relationship with their mentor.

Accept your mentor's flaws from the beginning of the relationship. Don't ignore or rationalize them. Mayor Daley and Al Eicoff were not perfect, but Howie and I accepted their imperfections early on, which allowed us to maintain our relationships with them over time and continue to learn from them.

HOW MENTORS CAN HELP YOUR CAREER

Mentors help mentees become successful, and they do so in many ways. They are particularly useful to people who come into an organization without any particular advantage—people who aren't viewed as high potentials, who lack connections in the company, or are not sophisticated about how to play politics. In other words, they are at a competitive disadvantage. Most of the people I interviewed talked about how a mentor leveled the playing field, providing them with everything from information to ideas that helped them succeed, either at the job they had or later in their careers.

Let's look at the three ways that mentors can best help you:

1. DEFEND YOU AGAINST YOUR ENEMIES.

Some people in your organization may view you as not smart enough, not connected enough, or not sufficiently polished. They may resent your existence and especially your success. They would prefer that "one of their own" have the position you have. Whether they are your colleagues or your superiors, their animosity can cause you problems. A mentor can defend you against these individuals. If your mentor is sufficiently powerful, her mere mentorship should protect you. In other instances, she may need to intervene directly on your behalf.

In an ideal world everyone would be happy for your triumphs and celebrate your achievements. But in reality, it's likely that a minority will view you as an outsider and resent your insider status.

Unfortunately, they may be a powerful minority. Denise joined a midsize entrepreneurial organization after spending two years working for a family business. The company had a hard-charging, wheeling-and-dealing culture, and some in the male-dominated executive group didn't think much of Denise. She was on the quiet side, and certainly didn't possess the macho swagger they exhibited. The CEO, though, thought Denise was terrific. He saw that she was able to sell with empathy rather than just with force, and he also realized the business was changing and Denise's approach was well-suited to the new direction. As a result, he defended Denise against the indirect and sometimes direct attacks against her, and she eventually became the number two person in the company.

2. OFFER SUPPORT.

Bill McCabe was a proofreader when he joined A. Eicoff & Co. I saw that he worked hard and smart, and he was a great guy. When I started to mentor him, though, Bill was resistant. Though he was ambitious, he was also insecure, in part because he was starting out as a proofreader. At first, he responded to his own insecurity by picking fights. I would say black, and he would say white. It was almost a reflex, and he ended up trying to defend indefensible positions. Over time, though, Bill made great strides and eventually took on a management role. While Bill was able to bring in new business, he was not as successful managing people. He would be too tough on them, setting unrealistically high performance standards and criticizing them when they couldn't meet these standards. As a result, some of his people were more concerned about being criticized than finding ways to improve their performance.

I supported Bill as he grew as an executive. From my standpoint, support meant being willing to listen and discuss any topic without repercussions. Bill knew that he could come to me with problems, and that I wouldn't hold his problems against him. He recognized that he could trust me, and that trust helped him to be honest with himself. By reflecting on our conversations and his own behavior, Bill was able to stop being so combative and tough. He lightened up, recognizing when to admit he was wrong and when to cut people some slack. Eventually, Bill became one of our top executives.

Mentors provide support through their willingness to listen and talk without judgment. If you're insecure or feel that others are better qualified than you are, you're going to need someone to turn to when you face problems and are worried about your abilities. Good mentors will let you be honest with them and with yourself. They help you regain your confidence, enabling you to see both your weaknesses and your strengths.

A mentor can also provide public as well as private support. Shortly after Ogilvy acquired the Eicoff agency I was invited to go to Monaco to participate in Ogilvy's heads-of-office annual meeting. Right from the start we were treated like royalty. Ogilvy management instructed me to fly first class from Chicago to Nice, a private helicopter ferried me from Nice to Monaco, and I was then picked up in a limousine and taken to the Hôtel de Paris, where I was given a luxurious room and money to gamble with in the casinos.

The heads-of-office meeting was held in the magnificent Princess Grace meeting room. Celestial light streamed in through skylights, plush carpeting made you feel like you were floating with each step, and the theme from *Chariots of Fire* poured out of speakers and announced our entrance.

The first day of the meeting I listened intently but said nothing. We sat in front of microphones bolted into the tables, and everyone's voice seemed amplified and godlike. A number of the speakers spoke brilliantly and passionately. Top Ogilvy executives

Bill Phillips and Norm Barry provided insights into advertising, and they did so with great eloquence. These were the stars not only of Ogilvy but of the entire advertising industry.

The subject of the second day was how to train creatives, and it was a subject on which I could speak with confidence. I was reluctant to speak, though, because I was the new guy surrounded by these advertising legends. But I had a point of view that no one else was expressing, and I thought I might introduce a provocative notion based on my direct-response experience. Back then, most of the Ogilvy offices were just starting or considering starting direct-response divisions. It struck me that I had something valuable to contribute, and it might be a good way to introduce myself to the group.

I cleared my throat, Ogilvy's Ken Roman immediately recognized me and every eye in the room fixed on me.

"If you really want to teach your creatives the power of advertising, take your stars and let them work in a direct-response group. Let them see the difference headlines and body copy make in the response they get from an ad. Let them do more than be creative for creative's sake . . ."

"BOOM, BOOM, BOOM."

It sounded like a series of small explosions. For the life of me, I couldn't figure out what was making this loud noise. My eyes darted around the room, and then, to my horror, I saw that the person making the noise was David Ogilvy himself. Or rather his microphone was making this noise as he stood and pulled violently at its neck, trying to lift it to his lips, apparently not realizing it was bolted to the table. His red face was a perfect match for his red suspenders.

What had I done? In that moment I was sure my career was over. Somehow I had offended him, and I was doomed.

And then he spoke, his rich Scottish accent making each word sound bronzed: "Thank God there's someone in this bloody company who finally agrees with me!"

In that moment everything changed. I went from outsider to insider with those thirteen supportive words. David Ogilvy was on my side—or rather I was on his—and there was no one better to have on your team than David. After the meeting ended, he sought me out, complimented me again, and insisted that I accompany him on a walk around Monaco. As valuable as his advice was as we walked, even more important were his public and private displays of support.

3. PROVIDE GUIDANCE THROUGH WORD AND DEED.

Mentors are not going to tell you how to solve all your problems or give you the secret formula for success. What they will do is share their hard-won wisdom. They can talk about situations similar to the ones you face and suggest what they or other people did to deal effectively with these situations. They can offer you inside information about how to deal with particular individuals and idiosyncrasies of your organization.

Perhaps more important, however, they give you the chance to observe them in action. Art Frigo draws the analogy between being mentored and an apprenticeship, and it is apt: You're allowed to watch a master craftsman practice his trade. This is especially important if you feel uncertain about how you should act in a corporate setting, about the right and wrong way of solving problems.

I picked up a lot by watching Al Eicoff in action. I remember meeting with a large client, Brunswick Corporation, to talk about a new agricultural product they had developed, a spray designed to keep the flies off cows. They had a large advertising budget to promote this product, and no doubt some agencies would have accepted the product with no questions asked.

Not Al. He wanted to know how effective the spray was. Eighty percent effective, he was told.

"You'll never sell it," Al replied. He then explained his rationale: If a farmer sprays his cow, he won't see the eighty flies lying dead on the ground; he'll notice the twenty flies still buzzing around his cow. In the mind of the farmer, the product will be deemed ineffective.

Al taught me the value of being honest with clients, even if it meant a short-term loss. If he had been dishonest, he might have received the assignment, but when the advertising didn't work he would also have received the blame. Certainly Al could have told me that honesty was the best policy. But seeing the lesson played out in front of my eyes was a far better learning experience than a mere statement of principle.

I'll leave the last word on the subject of mentors to Becky Jewett: "I have always prided myself on being a mentor for young people like my mentor was for me. This is one of the greatest opportunities leaders have, to give people opportunities, to see them blossom and change their lives."

CHAPTER 2

TRUST YOUR INSTINCT

How did Norm Bobins, now CEO of LaSalle Bank, know that he should leave his secure executive position at American National Bank—a place where he had worked for fourteen years—and join Exchange National Bank, a much smaller bank?

How did CDW (formerly known as Computer Discount Warehouse) founder Mike Krasny know that if he placed an ad in a magazine selling a used computer, he would tap into a largely untapped market?

How did Lettuce Entertain You Enterprises founder and chairman Rich Melman know that he should stick with a new type of restaurant—one designed with young, hip people in mind—when it was largely empty in its opening months?

They didn't actually "know." It wasn't a purely cognitive process that caused them to make these decisions. While they certainly used logic and analysis to help them decide, they relied on something else. Call it a hunch. Call it going with your gut. Call it trusting your instinct.

Just about all the high achievers I have interviewed mentioned this trait as crucial to their success. Sometimes trusting their gut caused them to ignore the conventional wisdom and do what they thought was right. Other times, their instincts led them to take risks in their jobs, careers, and businesses that on the surface seemed irrational. In the vast majority of instances, though, instinct proved to be a reliable guide.

I've trusted my instinct throughout my career; my mentor Al Eicoff was one of the most instinctive businesspeople I've ever met. Both of us, along with many others who may not have been the smartest or the most privileged, have used this inner quality well. As we'll see, C students tend to develop their instincts, while A students often let them languish.

Perhaps you're aware of *The Smartest Guys in the Room,* a book and a movie about Enron's leaders and how they destroyed their company. Enron's leaders were intellectually brilliant, creating an ingenious strategy that produced huge profits. As smart as Enron's leaders were, however, they did not trust their instincts. Instead, they trusted their brains and egos, which told them that they could get away with anything because they were smarter than everyone else. Yes, they were greedy and arrogant, but if they had paid attention to that little voice in their heads, they might have been able to manage their worst tendencies. Instinct can help people make tough choices, and that includes knowing when to back off from highly profitable tactics that are also highly unethical.

WHAT INSTINCT IS AND WHY IT IS SO IMPORTANT FOR C STUDENTS

Instinct isn't easy to define, but sports can provide a good analogy to help you understand how it operates. Many of the high achievers in these pages played high school and college sports, and several of them referred to their instincts in athletic terms. They talked about knowing when to punt and when to take their shot. They had to make split-second decisions as quarterbacks, batters, and point guards that directly affected the outcome of their games, allowing them to develop and trust their instincts. Instinct, then, helped them take the right actions when they didn't have much time for thought or analysis.

For purposes of this discussion, instinct is nothing more than an inner signal of what to do in a given situation. Most of us are taught to think before we act, but in sports, athletes are often criticized for thinking too much and thereby not taking advantage of their natural abilities. You've probably heard an athlete who breaks out of a slump say something like, "I stopped thinking so much and just started playing."

In team sports, instinct can also be used to make judgments about other people. When I played baseball, I knew instinctively who I could count on to make a play. They were the people who wanted to be at bat with the score tied in the bottom of the ninth or who wanted the ball hit to them in the last inning when we were leading by a run and the bases were loaded.

In the world of jobs and careers, trusting your instinct often becomes critical when making decisions about people. Recognizing who to partner with, who to delegate important jobs to, who to share important information with, who to turn to when you need help—instinct helps us read people in ways that observation and knowledge can't. As important as it is to know a person's track record and see them in action, it is often only part of the story. Some people can put on a good show, and it might seem as if they would make excellent partners or great hires, but appearances can be deceiving. That's why before making decisions about people, you need to pay attention to how you feel about the other person.

I have found that individuals who have had great academic success because of their analytical abilities can become overly dependent on data and logic to make decisions. They are great at analyzing the pros and cons, at researching their options and then choosing the option that comes out ahead. Sometimes this type of analysis is appropriate. Sometimes, however, analysis alone won't tell you the right thing to do.

In 1977, I was at a key point in my career. A. Eicoff & Co. was doing well, and as the number two person at the agency, my fate was tied to the agency's performance. At the time we had a large account, TV Magic Cards, an incredibly successful product that took advantage of the magic craze that was popular then. I had established a good relationship with the company's president, Rick Carey, in the previous four years that we had the account. In fact, when Rick was looking for a purchasing manager, I had recommended a guy I knew, Ed Green. Rick had hired him and was very happy with Ed's skills. The account was spending a lot of money with us, I liked their people, and their future looked rosy.

Until one Saturday night when the phone rang and it was Ed Green. My family and I had just ordered pizzas, the movie *Auntie Mame* was on television, and I was looking forward to a pleasant evening when Ed said he needed to come to my house and talk to me. I told him that was fine. When he arrived, he said, "You got me this job so I owe you. TV Magic is going bankrupt. We overbought and we're going to get a lot of merchandise returned, so we're not going to be able to pay your bill."

If they did not pay their bill, they would take the agency down with them. They were a big account and owed us a lot of money. The next day I met with Al Eicoff and told him what Ed had said. He turned white—he knew we had two choices, and both could spell disaster. One choice was to terminate the relationship with TV Magic Cards immediately. But if we did that, we would start a chain of events that probably would throw the company into bankruptcy sooner rather than later and we would never be paid what we were owed. On the other hand, if we continued the relationship and continued to buy time for TV Magic, we would increase their debt to us. Rather than incurring a significant but sustainable loss, we would incur the type of loss that would sink us.

To his credit, Al didn't make the decision. He knew that I was more familiar with the account than he was, and so he asked, "What should we do?"

Thinking about it logically, I had no answer. But my instinct told me that Rick was a decent person who would honor his commitments. I should emphasize that I had no hard evidence to back this belief. Though he had been a client for four years, Rick wasn't a close friend; I didn't know him well enough to be certain that I was right about him. Instinctively, though, I felt I was right and that he deserved a chance. So I said to Al, "Rick is an honorable guy. He'll find some way to pay us."

Al trusted me, and I trusted Rick. A few years later, TV Magic Cards went bankrupt, but Rick managed to pay almost all of his bill long before they went under. If I had been wrong, I could have destroyed the ad agency. Fortunately, my instincts were right.

Everyone has instincts, but not everyone develops them. C students tend to be more adept than others at not only developing them, but trusting them. A students become accustomed to relying on their brains to get ahead. They often achieve by using what they know, not what they sense or feel. As a result, they have trouble getting in touch with their gut responses and lack a sensitivity to what their gut is telling them.

Most C students, on the other hand, have gone through life operating by the seat of their pants. In school, when confronted by a teacher asking where their homework is, they have had to come up with a credible answer on the spot. To do decently on exams they didn't study for or in their worst subjects, they have had to depend on their ability to invent the right answers. Then, when their less than stellar academic record is brought up on a job interview, they have to think on their feet and sense the best argument to sell themselves.

This instinctive development takes place in anyone who doesn't have a smooth and easy sail from school into their careers. The concept of women's intuition may sound dubious to some, but women are often more adept than men at following their own impulses rather than the dictates of male-dominated organizations. Having encountered glass ceilings once too often, they learn to trust their gut in order to survive and thrive in companies that subtly discriminate against women. Late starters and others whose careers have begun inauspiciously are often forced to fall back on their instincts to navigate alternative paths through organizations. Confronted with questions about what they have been doing for the last five years or why they switched jobs so many times, they learn to sell themselves through instinctive responses to their interviewers. Many times, they trust their gut and tell the truth, even if it might suggest that they have been uncertain about their career in the past.

Ultimately, C students need to capitalize on their instincts. Other people may be able to get by on brainpower alone, but individuals who weren't blessed with genius IQs need to develop other strengths. Trusting their instincts can help them gain the confidence they might not otherwise have. Many people who fall into the broad C-student category have had their confidence shaken by less than perfect grades; job rejections; criticism from parents, spouses, and others; and discrimination because of their age, race, gender, or personal idiosyncrasies.

Instinct helps them overcome past rejections and failures. Flip Filipowski probably trusts his instinct as much as any person I've ever met. Though he grew up in a blue-collar environment and never finished college, he learned early that his instincts would lead him in the right direction. Consider that he founded start-up software company Platinum Technology in 1987, competing against Harvard MBAs and Silicon Valley high-tech gurus. Unintimidated, Flip had built the eighth-largest software company in the world by 1999 with revenues of $1 billion, and soon after sold it for $4 billion. Over the years, he has acquired more than two hundred companies and pioneered precedent-setting combinations of high-tech organizations that have been controversial, to say the least. While not all of Flip's ventures have been successful, he is undeterred by failure.

Flip says he learned to trust his instincts early on, and acting on instinct gives him the confidence to take on projects that reason alone might have discouraged him from tackling. He says, "What helped me to be so successful are the same things that get me in trouble—fearlessness, the ability to take on any amount of risk with no fear, the ability to face that risk with no panic, to persevere regardless of how many failures I've had. The person who keeps coming to bat and never gives up no matter what the disaster is the guy who wins. Never ever give up, no matter how beat up you are.

"When DBMS [one of the companies Flip founded] was taken over by a hostile group, I was thrown out of the company and replaced by people from Disney. I owned 45 percent of the company at the time, and I took the certificate of ownership, tore it up, and threw it back at them. Then I started another company.

"I act instinctively. Sure, I calculate risks and odds, but I'm willing to take on projects with 51 percent chance of success or better, even if other people feel there's only a 5 percent chance of success. I'm able to intuit quickly, and I instinctively know if others have missed what I've seen. Even though it's still risky, I have a better-than-even chance of succeeding."

Not everyone can be Flip. Most people can't accept the degree of risk he's willing to live with. The point, though, is that trusting your gut can give you the confidence to act, whether it's as an entrepreneur or within a corporate setting.

HOW TO DEVELOP AND TRUST YOUR INSTINCT

Flip and many other high achievers seem to have developed their instincts unconsciously. They reflexively relied on them when they were facing difficult situations or tough decisions. I've found, though, that this process doesn't come naturally to everyone. Many people have been brainwashed into believing that they should only trust their logic and the data. Because C students are often highly instinctive growing up and tend to act before thinking, they've been told time and again, "Stop doing the first thing that comes to mind and start thinking about things before making your decisions." As a result, they may have suppressed their instincts. Based on my own experiences as well as those I've observed in others, here is a step-by-step guide for learning to develop and trust your instinct:

1. TAKE A CHANCE EVERY NOW AND THEN AND DO THINGS BECAUSE THEY FEEL LIKE THE RIGHT THINGS TO DO.

Retrain yourself to heed your own impulses. No doubt there have been times when something inside pushed you to take a certain course of action that had no rational explanation. You decided to bring an umbrella to work even though the forecast was for nice weather, and sure enough it rained later in the day, or something caused you to attend a conference you don't usually attend, and you met a contact at the conference who steered you toward a great job.

I'm not saying that you should obey every impulse and defy reason whenever you make a decision. I'm saying that every so often, practice doing things that feel right, even if you can't put into words why you're doing them.

When entrepreneur Art Frigo was in his twenties and working for 3M, he went back to school at night and took a course called Managerial Economics. Though Art had a degree in electrical engineering, he didn't view himself as just a tech guy. When he went to his college reunion, he listened to his former classmates talking about their MBAs and how much money they were making and the exciting careers they were pursuing. He recognized that he needed to take more business courses if he wanted to achieve a higher level of success, so he signed up for Managerial Economics. On the last day of class, the professor invited the students to join him for a beer at the bar across the street. Most of the students had no interest in taking him up on the offer, but Art and two others decided to go to the bar. Art had no clear purpose in going; he wasn't close to the professor or particularly enamored of the subject. Yet something told him to go, and so he went. The two other students had their beers and departed, but Art stayed and talked to the professor.

Art asked him how to get ahead in a career, and the professor gave him a few pieces of advice and concluded by saying, "Become an expert at something."

"Like what?" Art asked him.

The professor suggested sales forecasting. At that point sales forecasting was in its infancy as a discipline, but the professor told Art about a few university professors in the New York area who knew more than anyone about sales forecasting and product planning. Art signed up for their classes and learned everything he could. Within the year, Art was hired at a consulting firm in large part because of his sales forecasting knowledge. This knowledge proved valuable, as Art was placed on key projects that someone with his educational background and work experience otherwise might not have been selected for. Art did extremely well on the projects and became a top performer at the consulting firm. Looking back, Art said that without that expertise, he probably would have remained "a salesman with a territory." With it, his career took off and provided him with the money, connections, and knowledge necessary to become a highly successful entrepreneur.

2. DON'T GIVE IN TO YOUR FEAR.

We all have fears related to our jobs, and most C students I've met have more than most. We are afraid of being criticized by our bosses, of not receiving a promotion or bonus, and of being fired. While these fears are normal, they can also prevent us from responding to situations authentically. Instead of making decisions that feel right or saying exactly what we believe, we play it safe or say what we think others want us to say. In short, we push back our instincts out of fear.

People who play it safe all the time will never succeed . . . or they will succeed only up to a point, becoming middle managers but never moving higher. The ones who really make it—who become successful entrepreneurs, CEOs, and other high-achieving professionals—are those who take chances based on their instincts.

About seven years ago I interviewed a woman named Melissa Feamster. I was impressed with her, especially because she had taken the time to read Al Eicoff's book. As we were moving toward the end of the interview, she asked me how I had ended up at Eicoff. I told her that the story was in Al's book.

"No," she said, "it's not in there."

I insisted it was.

She insisted it wasn't. Melissa wasn't defensive or antagonistic about it, but she obviously believed she was right.

I suggested she might want to take a second and rethink what she was saying.

At this point, most people would have backed off during a job interview with the CEO and said something like, "Oh, I must have missed that part, sorry," or words to that effect. Melissa, though, refused to retract her statement.

"Okay," I said, "you asked for it." I rose from my chair, plucked Al's book *Or Your Money Back* from the bookshelf and began reading the relevant passage. As I started to read, though, Melissa told me that that wasn't the book she had read.

It turned out she had read Al's second, lesser-known, book, which focused on the technical aspects of direct-response television advertising.

I strongly recommended that the agency hire Melissa, and not only was she hired, she turned out to be a great addition to the account staff. I knew she would be terrific, as soon as I realized that she had trusted her instinct rather than bow to the fear of antagonizing a prospective employer.

3. USE OBSERVATION TO CONFIRM YOUR INSTINCT.

To encourage yourself to trust your gut, use your powers of observation to confirm whether doing so is a good idea. If you act only on instinct, you're not using all the tools available to you. Instinct isn't infallible, so you want to use it judiciously. It's great when you respond positively to a presentation from a vendor—you instinctively feel that she is someone you can have a great business relationship with—but you should also pay attention to observable details and see if they confirm your instinct. Does the presenter make good eye contact? Does she speak in a way that feels sincere and honest? Answering these types of questions will go a long way toward telling you whether your instinct is right on the money.

When Becky Jewett, former chairman of the Direct Marketing Association's board of directors and CEO of a number of major-companies, was working for Talbots, a large apparel retailer and catalog company, she was contacted by a much smaller clothing catalog company, Chadwick's of Boston. She interviewed with the CEO of the company that owned Chadwick's and was offered the job of president. Analyzed logically, it was not the type of offer for which you would leave a major company like Talbots. The CEO was giving her two years to turn Chadwick's around, so the risk of failure was significant.

Nonetheless, Becky said, "I was really ready for it. I trusted my instincts. I was ready for the challenge, even though it was a smaller company."

Something told her that this was the right job for her, but she confirmed this gut response through observation. She connected with the parent company's CEO in a big way; she also looked at her situation at Talbots—she was working for her third boss in four years—and she saw the turnaround situation as the type of challenge she relished more than the more corporate role she had at Talbots.

These observations helped her follow her gut and accept the Chadwick's position. In five years she took the company from $75 million in sales to $550 million, and this turnaround made her reputation.

In the same way, when Ogilvy & Mather was negotiating to acquire Eicoff, my instinctive reaction was positive, but I still had doubts. I knew things were going to change, and I was not sure how well I or the Eicoff agency would adapt to life as part of a large corporation. If I had wanted to, I could have found a similar CEO position at a smaller, independent agency. Logically, this was the business life I had known and the environment in which I had thrived. Yet my instinct said stay with it, and my observations reinforced this conclusion. Specifically, I observed Ogilvy CEO Bill Phillips in action. Perhaps the most telling observation was an elevator ride I took with him at Ogilvy's New York headquarters. CEOs often seem to have a protective shield surrounding them in the elevator. They may talk to the person they're riding the elevator with, but everyone else gives them a wide berth, refraining from speaking to them or even looking at them.

Bill, though, talked to everyone, and everyone talked to him. At almost every stop the elevator made, someone would come on and Bill would clearly know the person and be aware of the account he was working on. Not only would Bill ask questions, but people were sufficiently comfortable to ask him questions as well. Ultimately, I figured that if my observations were correct, Bill ran an agency at which the people at Eicoff and I would feel at home. Combined with my instinct, I had faith that things would work out, and I decided that the acquisition would be beneficial for everyone involved.

JUDGING PEOPLE, CHOOSING JOBS, MAKING BUSINESS DECISIONS: HOW TO USE INSTINCT TO YOUR ADVANTAGE

In just about every large organization you'll find extraordinarily smart people who have made it to a certain level and will never make it further. As skilled as they are at their jobs, they lack a certain something. A brilliant MIS manager may not be very good at forming and sustaining solid business relationships. A genius at strategy may be too cerebral and introspective to be an inspiring leader. A McKinsey-trained executive may make great choices about programs and processes but continuously make poor decisions regarding his own career.

Very smart people are not always very good at hiring the right people, choosing business partners, or making astute career decisions. In large part, that's because they don't use their instinct to their advantage. They rely too much on their brains and not enough on their gut. As a result, they don't have a feel for the business, for the people they work with, or for how to motivate their employees.

C students who develop and trust their instincts can capitalize on their instincts in three areas: judging people, choosing jobs, and making business decisions. Let's look at each area.

A students who have been grouped with the academic elite from the time they started school have been raised to seek out those with similar backgrounds. They may be good at creating strong relationships with people who are just like them, but they are ill-prepared to deal with a diversity of individuals. They have always been academically segregated, and this can have an effect on how they relate to people. Some A students have been encouraged to rely exclusively on their brains, and they lack the instinct to adapt to a given individual, to sense when an aggressive approach would work with one person and a softer approach would work with another. They are unable to read a colleague or customer to figure out if they are reliable and honest or if they just talk a good game.

When you develop and trust your instinct, though, you are much more likely to form productive relationships with the right people. Joan, for instance, has become a consultant with a national reputation and an author of well-regarded books because of her instinct for people. Joan's career started slowly—she was a C plus or B minus student who went to law school after college but early on realized that she neither liked nor was particularly good at the law. Her instinct told her to try something else, so she opened her own consulting firm, without a clear idea of what its focus would be. At first, she tried a number of different areas of specialization, none of which were particularly successful. During this time, however, Joan made an effort to meet as many people as possible to develop strong contacts. She attended trade shows, seminars, corporate-sponsored cocktail parties, and other functions in order to make these contacts. Joan discovered that she enjoyed this networking process and was amazingly adept at identifying and forming relationships with the right people— individuals with whom she shared common values and business interests. Shortly after forming a critical mass of solid relationships, she started getting referrals for consulting projects. Many of these projects involved helping executives build productive relationships with their own people as well as alliances with vendors, community groups, and other external entities. Joan developed a reputation as a "matchmaker"—she was skilled at bringing together people with like-minded approaches and complementary skills who could help one another achieve business goals. Certainly part of Joan's matchmaking ability came from her ability to analyze individuals and make logical assumptions about who would work well together. Part if it, though, came from Joan's ability to trust her instinct when it came to people. On more than one occasion she would bring two individuals or groups together and say, "I just have a sense that you're going to find a project to work on together." Her prediction didn't always come true, but more often than not her instincts paid off for her clients.

Now I'll share with you one of my favorite stories, one that demonstrates why sometimes you should trust your instinct about people even when your brain is sending you the opposite message.

Some years ago, as I was sitting in my office, I was buzzed and told that a Brad Martin was on the phone. I didn't know any Brad Martin, but I took the call anyway.

"Brad Martin, Dallas, Texas, here," the blustery, drawling voice announced.

"What can I do for you?"

"I want to see you!" he said like a loan shark talking to a slow-paying customer.

I asked him when he wanted to meet.

"Tomorrow morning at nine A.M."

I explained I was busy at nine o'clock, but I could see him at ten.

"I'll be there," he said, and slammed the phone down.

During our conversation my brain was telling me that I wanted nothing to do with someone who was so belligerent. I was certain that the meeting would be a waste of time. Yet something prevented me from brushing off Brad. I couldn't articulate what it was at the time—maybe I chalked it up to curiosity—but I was there when he arrived the next morning.

He looked exactly as he sounded: a huge body with a dispro-portionately small head, wearing a white shirt pockmarked with tiny brown holes, the result of smoking a pipe and not paying at-tention to where the burning ashes dropped. He carried a large briefcase and followed me into the conference room.

When we were seated, he opened the briefcase to reveal a package labeled "Linen Curlers."

"What are those?" I asked.

"Can't you read?" he drawled, looking at me like I was a moron.

"I know what it says, but what do they do?"

"Women put them in their hair instead of rollers, only they're soft."

I asked him how much he was selling them for.

Twenty-four for eight dollars was his answer (which doesn't seem like much now, but was relatively costly then).

I told him I didn't think we could create commercials to sell the product profitably at that price.

"I heard you people were the best," he said, staring at me with a contempt that belied the compliment. "Anyone around here with any brains?"

That should have been enough. He was insulting and his product was not priced in a way that I thought it could sell. Every rational bone in my body was telling me to end the meeting and find a way to get him to leave before he went berserk. Instead, I left the conference room, found three people from our creative department, and asked them to look at Brad's product and give him their opinion. Brad gave them his pitch, and I asked if anyone thought we could sell his product effectively for eight dollars. All three of them said no.

"Y'all don't know what the hell you're talking about," he said.

I asked him what made him think a woman would be willing to pay eight dollars.

Brad turned to Carol Darr, a copywriter and the only woman in the room, and said, "'Cause they can screw in 'em. Tell them, honey."

Carol didn't know how to answer and mumbled she didn't wear rollers.

At that point, I figured it was time to end the meeting, and I did so by explaining that the agency had stringent credit requirements.

"I know what you're getting at," he said, and began searching through his pockets, pulling out various pieces of paper and pens until he found a blank piece of paper and a pen that worked. He wrote down two numbers and said they were for two banks in Texas; I should ask them about Brad Martin.

After he left, I did so. When I talked to the president of the first bank, he asked me how much credit we were thinking about extending to him. I said it might be as much as $75,000.

"You can easily add two zeroes to that figure and you'd still be fine."

I heard the same response from the second banker.

We eventually took Brad and his Linen Curlers on as a client, and it proved to be a great success, whether because of Brad's theory about women and sex or because they were a comfortable alternative to metal rollers, I'm not sure.

What I am sure of, however, is that my instinct said to give Brad as much rope as possible. Despite the negative first impression, something about him struck me as positive. Unconsciously, perhaps, I decided that I would hear him out and take a chance on someone who was not a typical ad agency client and who did not have a product that seemed viable. With hindsight, I think what my instinct was telling me was don't judge a book by its cover. Despite Brad's gruff exterior, he was actually a very smart businessman and a decent person.

Instinct can also be a great advantage in making on-the-job decisions. Some decisions—from whether to hire, fire, or promote to choosing between one supplier and another—are no-brainers, decided by pure logic. Other choices, though, occupy a gray area or have to be made in a split second. Many of the business leaders I know have had to make decisions without much information and with even less time for deliberation and analysis. In these situations instinct is crucial. When there's no obvious right answer, you have to go with your gut.

Dennis Bookshester, former CEO of department store, mail order, and specialty store retailer Carson Pirie Scott, possesses unerringly accurate instincts. When a growing number of professional women began returning to the workforce after having children in the 1980s, Dennis pioneered Carson's Corporate Level, a store-within-a-store concept that catered to the needs of these women. Anticipating that working women with kids would have significant time constraints, he fashioned Corporate Level to get these shoppers in and out as quickly as possible and provide them with the advice they needed to choose the right clothes at the right price. It was a huge success.

Though Dennis had information about the working woman trend that demonstrated Corporate Level was a wise idea, he also was relying on his instinct. There were 101 alternatives to Corporate Level that would have also capitalized on this trend, but Dennis chose Corporate Level because it made intuitive sense to him. As he told me, "You 'know' what the right thing is to do, and a lot of great results start with instinct. If you have an idea for something and it comes back to you—somebody else you work with has roughly the same idea—then it confirms your instinctive response."

Choosing a job or making a related type of career decision is the third area in which instinct can be invaluable. Top students from top schools and people with an "in" are going to receive plum job offers. They are more likely to receive fast-track status and have relatively easy choices to make. The rest of us aren't so lucky. For instance, we might have to make a choice between a job that offers more money but less possibility of career advancement and one that pays less money but provides more career opportunity. Many high achievers have faced bewildering choices about which job to take, whether to transfer to another division, if they should switch careers, and so on. When it seems impossible to choose between option A and option B, instinct can be useful.

Mike Waters is now a highly successful inventor and marketer of products such as LitterMaid as well as high-powered LED devices, patented propane heaters, and safety valves, but no one would have predicted his success based on his performance in school. In fact, his performance was so dismal that his parents had him take an IQ test to see if he was inherently slow. He did fine on the test—he simply was uninterested in academics and found the school environment stifling. What he loved to do was tinker with things—he would take apart the lawnmower and put it back together for fun—but this mechanical aptitude didn't help him get good grades. He managed to get through college and found employment in his father's company. It was a safe environment and one where Mike could do fine because he was the boss's son. Mike's instincts, though, screamed at him to do something else.

While he was working for his father he was temporarily placed in an engineering position. The person who had the job had had a nervous breakdown. Even though he lacked an engineering background, Mike knew enough about the product that he was given the job. He discovered that the tinkering skills he demonstrated while growing up translated into engineering aptitude. Using this aptitude was exciting, but he was soon moved into another position that didn't require this skill.

After his father died, he made the decision to leave the company and start something on his own. He created his own business model: He would design a product, build a company around it, and then sell it at a profit. It was the ideal job for someone who loved tinkering. It also was a tremendously risky model. Common sense would have dictated that Mike ease into this goal by going back to school, getting a degree, and then working for someone else designing products before he designed on his own dime. Mike's gut, on the other hand, told him that he was ready to put his model into practice, and shortly after he did, he had his first big success. Over the years, he has designed and built companies around plastics machinery, industrial computer controls, pet products, and eyeglasses. Each time, his instinct combined with his design genius has helped him create highly innovative, highly marketable products.

Mike Waters and the others profiled here succeeded for reasons besides their instincts, but the ability to sense what they should do in a given situation has been at least as valuable as facts and figures. Whether you are struggling with decisions about people, job choices, or business issues, give yourself permission to trust your instincts. They may not be right all the time, but for C students in particular, they may give you a competitive advantage over less instinctive A students.

CHAPTER 3

STRIVE TO BE A BETTER PERSON THAN AN EMPLOYEE

C ontrary to what you may have heard, nice guys don't finish last. Not everyone can be a rocket scientist. Not
everyone can go to Harvard. But everyone is capable of
being an honest, decent human being, and if you make an effort
to display your good qualities in work environments, it will make
your reputation and possibly your career.

There is a myth in the business world that the people who
reach the top are ruthless, heartless, and egotistical; that you have
to be manipulative and obsessive if you're going to succeed in a
cutthroat corporate environment. In fact, the higher you go in
most organizations, the nicer the people are. Certainly there are
exceptions to this rule. Some companies are myopically focused
on short-term performance and any type of behavior is acceptable
to achieve the goal. If you're a C student, though, you don't want
to work there.

You do want to work where qualities such as honesty, compassion, loyalty, and courtesy are valued. In these environments people are going to think about you in one of two ways. As a matter
of fact, you probably think about others in the same two ways.
When you are asked about an individual you worked with, or
even one of your friends, how do you respond? No matter what

else you might say about this person, you're likely to conclude with "He's a good guy" or "He's a bad guy."

Good guys are the ones who generally get hired and promoted; they're the ones people want to do business with. Bad guys, on the other hand, are looked at warily. They are passed over for jobs in which people skills are important, and even the most talented of these individuals often hit "character ceilings," rising to a certain level but no higher.

Given all this, it's in your best interest to be the good person you are rather than feel you have to play the part of the ruthless professional. Good, though, is open to interpretation, so let's start out by defining our terms.

GOOD DOES NOT MEAN PUSHOVER

The feedback I've received over the years tells me that I've been a caring and trustworthy CEO—these qualities mean a lot to me and I try and display them as much as possible. No one, however, would consider me a pushover. As any CEO knows, you can't do your job effectively unless you can make tough decisions and stand up for what you believe. Therefore, recognize that qualities such as honesty, empathy, and trust go hand in hand with traits such as toughness and courage. People combine toughness and decency in many different ways. Some of the individuals profiled in these pages have gruff exteriors but hearts of gold. Others are charming and kindhearted, but inside they're made of steel. All of them, though, have strong values, and in both their personal and professional lives they attempt to maintain high standards.

They also make a *consistent effort* to communicate their character in work situations. Those two words are italicized for a reason. Some people may be great spouses, parents, and members of their communities, but they don't demonstrate these positive qualities at work. Being a good person as a leader and as a professional requires conscious effort. It's not just steering clear of immoral or unethical actions, but also looking for ways to help others and make them feel valued.

Larry Levy, for instance, is known far and wide as a person who is extraordinarily honest and trustworthy. He makes an effort to keep his promises, whether it's a promise to a future business partner or someone who works for him. As an entrepreneur and dealmaker, his scrupulous honesty and high moral character may seem like anomalies, but Larry says that he learned the importance of reputation early on.

"I witnessed the previous generation of entrepreneurs, and some of them were pretty rotten guys. My dad was involved in the record business in the early days of rock and roll, and there were some bad people in that business. My dad wasn't like that, and I vowed not to be like that. I've refused to take shortcuts or cheat in any way. I'm very conscious of my integrity and of being a good person."

Being good doesn't mean being a goody two-shoes. People who are rigidly idealistic and haven't mastered the art of compromise will diminish their effectiveness. They come off as self-righteous and alienate colleagues with their holier than thou attitude. It's possible to be a decent human being at work without adopting inflexible, judgmental positions. The late Mayor Richard J. Daley taught former state senator Howie Carroll that in a business known for its corrupt participants—and during Mayor Daley's reign there were plenty of corrupt politicians—it was still possible to maintain a good name without being judgmental.

"The mayor told me that a leader cannot take a dime and should never do anything that might taint his reputation. He said that you had an obligation to both the party and the city, and that a good leader helps people. At the same time, the mayor may have done business with some people who were on the take, but he didn't judge. He drove home this point by telling me that there were people who worked for him who had problems with drink. He told me if I faced a similar situation, I should let them know that I know they drink. It was a way of showing disapproval without judgment. As he told me, 'You've got to be honest, but you've also got to be practical.'"

Someone who worked at A. Eicoff & Co. once described the agency as a "bunch of characters with character," and I think that description communicates what I'm advocating. You can be eccentric, feisty, aggressive, and mercurial and possess all sorts of other distinctive but ethically neutral traits. I would be the last person to suggest that you should be blandly nice or saintly. At the same time, though, you should take time to determine what you believe and why, and hold yourself accountable to these values. There are all sorts of ways to communicate your values through your behavior, but first let's look at how doing so benefits C students.

GIVE YOURSELF THE ADVANTAGE OF INTEGRITY, CHARACTER, AND EMPATHY

While being a decent human being is a good end in and of itself, it comes with a bonus. In today's world, relationship-building is a critical skill. Being able to communicate, motivate, listen, create trust, and earn respect all have a tremendous impact on your career and your effectiveness. More than ever, people who can resolve conflicts, build partnerships, and manage teams are worth their weight in gold. Leaders with these capacities tend not to be the brilliant strategists and genius technicians. Instead, they are regular folks, individuals with exceptional people skills and sterling character. More often than not they are C students.

As a C student, you are in a good situation to capitalize on the character you developed early in life. Receiving average grades is humbling, preventing you from getting too arrogant. You weren't obsessively competitive in school and were happy to share your class notes; you learned to be generous with your information and ideas. You probably also recognized the importance of leading a balanced life. While other people may have been academic grinds, spending hours every night in the library, you found a balance between studying and socializing. You formed great friendships and learned to communicate clearly and compellingly. Rather than feeling the need to dominate conversations and express your brilliant opinions, you were able to sit back, listen, and respond to what others said. You also discovered that people tend to judge you for who you are rather than what you know.

All this has prepared you to be a person of character in the workplace. If you work hard at displaying this character, you'll reap benefits in the following three ways:

1. PEOPLE WILL WANT TO WORK AND DO BUSINESS WITH YOU.

In just about any organization, people gravitate toward individuals who exude decency and charm. They naturally want to work with those who are fun to be around and who are able to listen as well as talk. They want to collaborate with colleagues who are flexible and able to recognize the value of ideas other people come up with. Customers and suppliers, too, will gravitate toward individuals they trust, whom they believe have their best interests at heart.

Rich Melman of Lettuce Entertain You Enterprises (LEYE) has done an amazing job of creating employee loyalty and building business relationships that last far longer than the norm in the notoriously volatile restaurant business. He has also established unusual customer loyalty for his restaurants. This has come about in large part because Rich has consistently emphasized honesty and decency, and it is one of the reasons LEYE has received awards, including *Chicago* magazine's number six ranking in its "Best Places to Work" survey and number one ranking in employee satisfaction.

Rich describes his philosophy as follows: "I'm brutally honest, though not mean-spirited. When someone needs to be told they're off base, I don't have a hard time doing it. Integrity comes about in many ways. Being honest with yourself. Being honest with others. Not cheating people. This is a strong and healthy part of our culture. Leaders work hard and are honest, and their people follow suit."

Over the years, LEYE has created over 130 restaurants. In some instances they have taken in partners for investing purposes, and it has been rare that those partners lost money. One time, though, LEYE tried a new restaurant concept that didn't work right away. They could have made some changes and continued to improve the concept, and odds were it would have made money eventually. During that rebuilding phase, though, the partners still would not have made back their initial investment. Though LEYE was under no contractual obligation to return the money to the partners, they did so and closed the restaurant. One of the investors ran into Rich shortly after the payout. When the investor introduced Rich to a friend he was with, the investor said of Rich, "Here's a guy who could have walked away from us, never given our money back, but he paid us back."

Rich said, "I just thought it was the right thing to do. I messed up. I should have conceived the restaurant differently so that it would have been more successful."

I suspect that this partner, as well as the others involved in the venture, would be eager to do business with Rich again.

People want to work with those who do the right thing, not just because it makes sense financially, but because these individuals are enjoyable to be around. No one likes to work with smug individuals or those who pontificate at the drop of a hat. Unethical and amoral individuals also turn people off. So, too, do people who are rude, crude, or antisocial in other ways. On the other hand, most people love to work with colleagues who are friendly, open, and honest. They want to be on teams with people they can depend on and with whom they enjoy spending time.

Throughout my career, I have tried to make as many friends and as few enemies as possible. My theory has always been that the more people you have rooting for you, the greater the chances of your success. I recognize that sometimes people will choose to work with a jerk because his skill is critical to a particular project or they'll hire a supplier who is arrogant but is also the best in the business. All things being equal, though, most people will choose to do business with someone they like over someone they don't trust or find unpleasant.

2. YOU WILL BE A CREDIBLE, TRUSTED LEADER.

Unfortunately, we live in a time when people place less trust in their leaders than ever before. CEOs at companies such as Enron, Tyco, and WorldCom have made the public in general and corporate employees specifically distrustful of top executives.

If you aspire to be a leader in your organization, I would recommend starting to develop your reputation as early as possible. Everyone begins work with a blank slate, and every day you enter

something on that slate that reflects on you positively or nega-
tively. Your reputation is cumulative, and if you have many more
positive than negative entries after a period of time, you'll position yourself for top jobs. As much as organizations want their
leaders to produce results, they also want them to present a solid-
citizen image to the public and inspire and motivate employees.
They want everyone to feel that a leader has their best interests at
heart, and that if she has to make a tough decision—downsizing,
selling off a division—employees will give her the benefit of the
doubt.

As a CEO for over twenty-five years, I have attempted to be a
trusted, accessible leader. I reinforce this image in many ways; for
example, I treat clerical people with the same respect I treat vice
presidents with; I communicate my intolerance of dishonest practices; and I work hard to understand other people's points of view.
I have also done everything possible to maintain my good name.
I was taught the value of a good name by my grandfather Charles
Fingeret. When I was a young boy, I used to walk with my grandfather from his Coraopolis scrap yard to the bank to deposit the
cash he had earned that week; he always carried what seemed to
me a big roll of cash, though it probably seemed so large because
there were so many ones. One day while we were on our walk, he
stopped at a shop on Mill Street called Joe Workman's to buy a Ben
Hogan hat, which cost about three dollars. My grandfather said to
the shop owner, "I don't have any money with me at the moment." The owner responded, "Don't worry, Charlie, we know
you're good for it."

When we walked out of the store, I asked him why he had told
the owner he didn't have any money.

"I wanted to show you the importance of having a good
name."

I never forgot the lesson my grandfather taught me that day.

3. YOUR ODDS OF GETTING JOB OFFERS AND RECEIVING PROMOTIONS WILL INCREASE.

When a company is looking at a job candidate, they first look to see if that person has the necessary experience and expertise to fit the job. Almost as important, though, is whether she has the right personality and values for the job. After interviewing a candidate, they might ask themselves the following questions:

- Is this person a good fit for our company? Will he get along well with others on his team?

- Does she seem as if she might be overly egotistic or self-serving? Does she possess an arrogance that might rub others the wrong way?

- Do I like this person? Did I enjoy talking to him during the interview, and did he listen and absorb what I said?

- Does this candidate seem as if she has good values, that she would work with suppliers and customers in an ethical manner?

Sometimes people mistakenly believe they should show off during job interviews, boasting of their accomplishments and demonstrating their superior knowledge. Typically, they talk too much and listen too little. It's fine to mention your accomplishments, but this can be done naturally within the course of a normal conversation. More often than not, boastful, smug job candidates turn off interviewers, who will think to themselves, "I can't stand this guy now; how is it going to be if I have to see him every day?"

In terms of promotions, one of the great myths is that the most qualified person gets promoted. If the promotion involves a highly technical position—an accounting or MIS job, for example—then expertise may be the single most important factor. If, on the other hand, the job involves a lot of people responsibilities, then other factors come into play. C students receive promotions to managerial jobs all the time because they know how to develop other people, and establish relationships with a wide range of people; they also are responsible and committed. A students may be promoted up to a certain level in technical departments—their superior computer design expertise secures a top job in that department—but they may not be considered seriously for higher-level positions involving numerous people responsibilities.

Tradeoffs inevitably must be made in both hiring and promoting. Sometimes organizations will be desperate for someone with the knowledge and skills to handle a challenging position, and this desperation may make them willing to hire someone who is not Mr. Personality. It is also true that most people won't hire or promote someone who lacks the skills or knowledge to handle a job, even if they are the nicest guy in the world. In many instances, though, allowing your natural integrity, charm, and humanity to show will make a big difference in your career.

HOW TO CAPITALIZE ON YOUR BEST QUALITIES

Having good qualities and capitalizing on them are two different things. My optimistic assumption is that you possess qualities such as honesty and diligence, and I'm further assuming that over the years you've been rewarded for hard work and ethical behavior at least as often as you've been rewarded for academic achievement. But whether you've allowed these positive qualities to show in the workplace is another question. I'm not suggesting that you would be purposefully manipulative or deceitful in order to get ahead. What I am suggesting is that many people are afraid to let their best qualities shine at work, assuming that it might make them appear soft. As a result, they don't reap the benefits just discussed.

To take advantage of your good qualities, follow these nine work strategies.

1. SHARE YOUR SUCCESS WITH OTHERS.

Some of the high achievers profiled here have downplayed their own achievements and insisted that they owe their success at least in part to the efforts of others. Their statements don't come across as false humility. Instead, they indicate their genuine gratitude for the contributions of colleagues and mentors and their belief that success is a group rather than an individual effort.

As CEO of Carson Pirie Scott, Dennis Bookshester enjoyed enormous success and received much praise for leading the retailer to record sales and profits. Throughout his tenure, though, Dennis made it his policy to include others in the spotlight and attribute significant achievements to colleagues. As he says, "You want to give credit to other people and never say, 'I did it myself.' Even if something is your idea, you should help the people who contributed recognize the role they played in making something work. I always recognized people for doing a great job, even when I may have come up with the idea originally."

2. BEND OVER BACKWARD TO WORK WELL WITH OTHERS.

It takes effort to be a productive collaborator. No doubt some people will rub you the wrong way and you will find it difficult to talk with them, let alone work with them. There will also be times when you feel that you can accomplish a goal faster by yourself than in a group. Recognize, though, that organizations are increasingly relying on teams to get things done. Being productive in team environments, therefore, is a highly marketable skill. You may have to swallow your pride at times or force yourself to adjust your schedule or style to accommodate other people, but it will be worth it. When you develop a reputation for being a good collaborator, you have a better chance of getting assigned to top teams working on your company's key business issues.

Sam Morasca of Shell attributes his success to his team skills. He says, "I always felt that you could be the smartest guy in world, but if you couldn't work well with other people and get them to see your side—and if you didn't listen to their side—you would have trouble. I did well with teams, and as a result I ended up being put on high-profile projects—the Saudi Arabian project, the Alaskan project, the Deep Water Tanker projects.

"I was a good team member because I'm a social person. I come from an Italian family, and I'm not a solo player. I also came from an athletic background, so I've been involved in team sports. Growing up, I preferred to be a team player than an individual star. When I became a senior person at Shell, though, all of a sudden I didn't have a team of peers. Nonetheless, I would roll up my sleeves and be there with the troops. Some of the old-timers viewed this with disapproval, but I would rather be eating pizza with my team than in the executive dining room."

3. FIND A CULTURE WHERE NICENESS COUNTS.

As I noted earlier, not every company is an ideal place for C students. The Leo Burnett agency was seriously pursuing Eicoff prior to its acquistion by Ogilvy & Mather. But Leo Burnett seemed to have a Darwinian culture, at least at the time. Young people were placed in the media department, and only the strong survived. To do well there, you had to be political, and I wouldn't have wanted any part of that culture. C students need to choose their cultures carefully. You're most likely to flourish in companies that are less political and more humanistic.

4. PRACTICE SMALL ACTS OF KINDNESS AND CONSIDERATION.

You don't have to be the professional equivalent of Mother Teresa to be considered a good gal or guy. You can't offer career-saving advice every day. You can, however, display good manners and treat people with small kindnesses regularly.

When I first arrived at Eicoff, I didn't understand the importance of being nice. I was twenty-seven and in a hurry to make my mark; I thought you had to be a tough guy to succeed. Al Eicoff, who looked and talked like a tough guy, recognized the importance of common courtesy. A number of employees had complained about my gruff demeanor, and Al took me aside and said, "In order to succeed here, you have to be nicer. For instance, if I want you to have a seat in that chair, I can do it one of two ways. First, I can say, 'SIT DOWN!!!' Or second, I can ask, 'Will you please sit down?' The first way, you want to kill me. The second way, you're receptive to what I have to tell you."

Here are some other ways of practicing small acts of kindness:

- Never summon people to your office. Bosses summon direct reports reflexively, and it creates low-level animosity that builds up over time. No one enjoys being treated like a slave. Summoning also gives people the impression that you think you're superior, detracting from all the other good things you might do. Therefore, either ask people to come to your office or stop by their office.

- Make your own phone calls whenever possible. Few things create a worse impression than a manager who has his secretary

make his calls for him, and then adds insult to injury by forcing the person on the other end to wait until he is ready to
take the call.

• Ask busy people what you can do to help. It may be your boss,
colleague, or direct report who seems overwhelmed and stressed
out. The least you can do is ask if you can assist her in any way.
It may be that there's nothing you can do, but the gesture will
be appreciated and remembered.

• Be friendly and polite when dealing with mailroom personnel,
clerical staff, and especially secretaries. I have never understood
why some professional people feel it's acceptable to treat non-
professional staff with disdain or indifference. I have found
that A students can be particularly guilty of this sin, acting like
these individuals aren't at their level, and thus they're not obli-
gated to behave civilly toward them. C students have a natural
appreciation of nonprofessionals—there but for the grace of
hard work and some lucky breaks go I—and so are more likely
to treat them with respect. Still, some C students forget how
they hated the disdain they felt from their "betters" and fall
into the trap of only being nice to the people who can help
them. Secretaries, in fact, can help you. They can also hurt you.
If you doubt it, just be rude to a secretary. At some point he'll
let his boss know that you weren't particularly nice. To a great
extent reputations are made or broken through the cumulative
comments of an organization's secretaries.

• Smile and say hello. Harried executives rushing from one
meeting to the next may brush past you without even a nod of
recognition. Their faces may be screwed up into frowns or gri-
maces, communicating that you don't want anything to do
with them at that moment. Avoid walking around in a funk or
wearing a mask of indifference. Smile at people and say hello,

even to top executives who may be frowning or grimacing. These small gestures give off good vibes, and good vibes are part of what builds your reputation.

- Say please and thank you. These little words mean a lot, especially if you say them consistently and to everyone regardless of rank. Saying thanks to a secretary for working overtime means just as much as thanking the boss for a promotion. It communicates that you're intrinsically a good person, not someone who is only nice when it serves her purposes. It drives me nuts when I hear one of my people say, "I need you to do this" as opposed to "Will you please do this?" The former communicates that you view the other person as a functionary, the latter that you see the other person as a real human being.

5. ESTABLISH SMALL BUT MEANINGFUL NONWORK CONNECTIONS.

Whether you're a CEO or just starting out in your career, you have more in common with people you work with than you assume. It may be that you attended the same college. You may have a mutual love of classical music or historical novels. You may both relish Thai cooking. Whatever it is, you can establish a quick connection to anyone by making small talk. It doesn't take more than a few questions to figure out where someone grew up, what school they attended, and the hobbies they enjoy.

By establishing this connection and referring to it when you see this coworker, you demonstrate that you were paying attention to what they had to say. Many people limit their communication to impersonal exchanges of information and fail to establish a human relationship. It may seem like a small thing, but making the personal connection can take the relationship to a more meaningful level. Instead of going into your coworker's office and saying, "Here's the report," handing it over, and leaving, you can start out the interaction by saying, "I can't believe how the White Sox third baseman blew that play in the eighth inning last night." Knowing that the report recipient is a rabid White Sox fan, you may spend the next ten minutes venting your mutual frustration. These sharing exchanges over time help you build a supportive network. When you're up for a promotion or in need of resources, people will want to help you because you've made these human connections.

6. BE GENUINE.

People can spot phony niceness a mile off. Don't try to be someone you're not, forcing laughter at jokes you don't find funny or buttering up people you think can assist your career. You don't need to censor your nice qualities. You don't have to hide your disappointment, contain your laughter, or mask your approval. Stop worrying about being professional and start worrying about being more of the person you are. Let people see your sense of humor, your idiosyncrasies, and your concerns. Be yourself, and the odds are that people will respond positively.

7. WHEN IN DOUBT, DO THE RIGHT THING.

No matter what your profession is or your position in it, you're going to be tempted to take shortcuts or do something that is less than honest. There are many morally gray areas. You may want to leave your company immediately for another position even if you've promised your boss you would never depart without giving her at least two weeks' notice. Your time is being consumed by the company's largest customer, so when a smaller customer needs some help, you tell your assistant, "Screw them; they're small fry; we need to devote ourselves to the big fish." Or you may have just offered a position to one candidate, and then learned that a more talented individual is interested in the job. Can you rescind the offer?

Doing the right thing can be difficult, but it's essential if you want to be known as a decent, caring person. I've found that C students generally know the right thing to do in most situations, but they rationalize doing the wrong thing. They tell themselves that it's just a small indiscretion or that their decision may hurt a few people short-term but help a greater number in the long run.

The key here is to examine your decision making for rationalizations. Trust your instinct to guide you in these instances. If you feel it's the wrong thing to do, go with your gut.

8. WHENEVER POSSIBLE, FORGIVE YOUR ENEMIES.

Some people don't deserve to be forgiven. At some point in your career, you're likely to encounter an individual who has it in for you and does something unforgivable. You don't want anything to do with this person, since it's unlikely he'll ever change. On the other hand, you're much more likely to encounter people who offend, irritate, and disappoint you. These individuals might not be bad people; they simply make mistakes in judgment. C students can use all the friends they can get, so don't burn bridges and avoid creating more enemies.

Bose Electronics has been one of our clients at Eicoff since 1992. After about seven years, our main client contact, Mark Rutherford, made the decision to fire us and replace us with another agency. The new agency promised Bose all sorts of things that they were unable to deliver. We heard that Mark wanted to rehire Eicoff, but he wasn't sure we would want to work with them again.

I was furious when Bose dropped us, since I felt we had done a good job for them. Nonetheless, I flew to Boston to meet with Mark. I told Mark, "It broke my heart when we lost you as an account, but I would walk from Chicago to Boston to get this account back. You just made a mistake, but that's in the past."

I could have made him feel guilty, exacting a small measure of vengeance for his mistake. I knew he wanted Eicoff back as his agency, and I had license to say whatever I wanted in this situation. Rubbing salt into the wound, however, would have done neither of us any good. I forgave him, and in doing so started building a great relationship with Mark that is still going strong even though he no longer works for Bose.

9. BE OPTIMISTIC.

I'm not telling you to be Pollyannaish or simpleminded in your optimism. Don't deny reality and pretend everything is great when it isn't. At the same time, no one likes a pessimist. In every organization you'll find very smart individuals who are also very cynical and sarcastic, who could watch a beautiful sunset and talk only about the dark night to come. People love working with those who see possibility and hope rather than impossibility and doom.

At this point, I'll turn the floor over to Sam Morasca, who can argue for optimism more ably than I can:

"My dad told me that the world doesn't like a grouch. At Shell everyone was smart. But people complained and criticized all the time without having a solution, and it was no fun working with these grouches.

"There is a story of a psychologist who tested two ten-year-old kids—one was an eternal optimist, and one was a pessimist. The psychologist put the pessimistic kid in a room with fancy toys and said, 'This room is yours, do anything you want, we'll be back in few hours.' He then put the optimistic kid in a room with just a pile of horse manure and a shovel. When the psychologist returned to the room with the pessimistic kid and the toys, he found the child sitting in the corner doing nothing. He complained he was bored, that he didn't know how to work all the toys, and that he was worried about breaking them. When the psychologist entered the optimistic kid's room, he found the boy whistling and shoveling the manure to the other side of the room. The psychologist asked him what he was doing. He said, 'With all this shit, there has to be a pony somewhere.'"

I don't know about you, but I'd rather have the kid with the shovel on my team.

CHAPTER 4

TAKE RESPONSIBILITY SERIOUSLY

There are people in every organization who are known for taking responsibility seriously. They are go-to people. As I walk down the corridors of my ad agency, I absolutely know who I can go to when I need a job done without complaints or excuses. They are the individuals who will volunteer for tasks no one else wants to do and will step up and take the blame if something doesn't work out. They are also the people who I am absolutely certain will give an assignment their best shot, no matter what it involves or even if they're not particularly excited about it.

People who are known for taking responsibility seriously aren't always the best and the brightest, but they are the ones every boss wants on her team. Responsible people are much more likely to receive promotions and attract and keep customers than people with technical or other organizational skills. There is no substitute for the person who is completely reliable and dogged in the pursuit of her goals.

This trait is one that C students can make their own. They can compete with people who may have a better education, greater expertise, or superior political skills by stepping up and saying, "I'll do it." In every company, you'll find very smart people who aren't very responsible. They are either lazy or feel that certain projects are beneath them. And while many employees are hard-working, many are scared of responsibility. They are afraid of failure, and taking on responsibility may mean taking responsibility for failing.

Many people pay lip service to being responsible, but they don't take their responsibilities seriously. You've probably heard a professional coach or athlete say that he takes complete responsibility for a loss, but you never believe for a minute that he's going to lose a minute's worth of sleep—or a dollar's worth of income—over the loss.

So what does taking responsibility mean in real-world terms? Let's look at what goes into being responsible and how to bring it into the workplace. To help you achieve this goal, I've included the five following tips.

1. DO WHATEVER TASK NEEDS DOING.

Mike Krasny gave me a great definition of responsibility when he talked about an incident early in his life in which he felt he had been irresponsible. When he was fourteen, he worked at a fast-food restaurant with four other kids. The owner chose him to lock the door when they closed, and Mike took a great deal of pride in this task. One night one of his coworkers told him that he would lock up. While Mike's impulse was to check the door, another kid told him not to worry about it, he had done it, and so Mike didn't double-check. The next morning the owner of the restaurant bawled him out because the door had been locked improperly. Mike felt terrible. He explained, "I took the responsibility seriously, and it bothered me that I let him down. In fact, it still bothers me to this day."

No doubt CDW's incredible success is largely the result of Mike taking responsibility for tasks few other CEOs would handle. In fact, it wouldn't be unusual to find Mike loading computers onto delivery trucks or repairing broken machines. His innate sense of responsibility makes him want to take on whatever task needs doing. He doesn't want to let anyone else down.

Obviously, time and job parameters prevent you from doing everything all the time. At the same time, you can be the first to say "I'll do it" regardless of the prestige of the assignment or how difficult it might be.

2. TAKE THE HEAT.

Craig Duchossois coined this term in relation to responsibility. As the CEO of one of Chicago's largest private companies, Craig has more than six thousand employees located all over the world. He acknowledges that it's inevitable that some of them will make mistakes. He also understands that it is human nature for people to "run for cover when things get hot." While Craig doesn't condone mistakes, he also doesn't feel that only the person who made the error should take the blame. He says that "a sign of a true leader is his understanding that he must take responsibility for the actions of subordinates." This means stepping up and enduring the criticism of bosses, customers, the media, or whoever is furious with a negative outcome. As Craig says, "We've all seen people who are insecure with themselves and looking for others to blame. To me that is anathema. It does no good for me to say I wasn't in China, I wasn't in Mexico, so I'm not responsible for what happened. I take the heat and stand behind my troops."

Craig is one of the most responsible leaders I know, as he is willing to share responsibility for mistakes made by subordinates in ways few CEOs are willing to do. Craig has a fierce belief in supporting his people, and he has been rewarded with extremely loyal, hardworking employees.

C students can also receive rewards by taking the heat when things go wrong. I'm not saying that you should take the blame when you had nothing to do with a screwup or that you should constantly say "mea culpa." Every so often, however, you're going to be involved in a project that goes awry, and you need to be willing to do some soul-searching and determine whether you contributed to the problem. If so, your willingness to accept responsibility will separate you from the rest of the project members. When you alone acknowledge how you contributed to a failure—and when you do so intelligently and perceptively—your ability to step forward and take some of the blame will be remembered in a positive way.

3. DO IT BECAUSE IT'S THE RIGHT THING TO DO.

You can take responsibility out of a sense of obligation, or you can do so on principle. In the former, you can tell your boss that you'll take a difficult assignment because you know that she expects you to tackle it and it would be difficult for you to refuse.

On the other hand, when you take responsibility on principle, it's done out of a sense of what's right. When you take responsibility based on your beliefs or principles, you often run the risk of negative consequences. For instance, many people in your organization might dislike the company's environmental policies, so you take the responsibility of stepping up and telling a top executive that you and others feel the company should do more to help clean up the environment. This may not endear you to management and may even cause some unenlightened executives to view you as a troublemaker. There will always be people who feel threatened by those who act on principle rather than out of obligation. But others will be impressed.

One of the biggest challenges I have faced as a CEO has to do with taking responsibility. I recall with great clarity—and still with a measure of shock—the day I learned we had inadvertently over-spent a major client's yearly budget by a six-figure sum. This was a double whammy: Not only would we lose revenue, which would affect our bonuses, but our client would probably fire us when we told them about the mistake. I should add that accidental overex-penditures happen every so often in the ad agency business, and in some instances agencies can "hide" the additional expenditures and the client is none the wiser.

Hiding this or any overexpenditure is never an option for me because it is just plain wrong. As much as I hated to make the call to the client, I took responsibility for the mistake. I still remember the feeling of dread as I held the phone to my ear and waited to hear our client contact's voice. I had to swallow my pride, admit that we failed them in the worst possible way, and vow that it would never happen again. Even though this was the right thing to do, it still felt terrible. Acting according to principle is not al-ways easy. I knew, though, that I had to do the right thing because I believe in an honest agency-client relationship. I also needed to set a good example to my own people. If we had papered over the mistake, I would have sent a message to everyone at Eicoff that we don't really care about clients; that when push comes to shove we take the easy way out. If other Eicoff executives faced a similar sit-uation, they, too, might have shirked responsibility based on my example.

4. VOLUNTEER FOR THE JOBS NO ONE ELSE WANTS.

C students can be intimidated by these jobs; they remind them of the extra-credit assignments in school that they used to shun. Unlike school, however, these work assignments have a large upside and usually no downside. When you volunteer for a distasteful or difficult job, even if you fail no one holds it against you. Everyone knows it was a job no one else wanted, so you still receive credit for stepping up and volunteering. If, however, you volunteer for a challenging assignment and generate a positive outcome, you become a hero. You not only took responsibility for volunteering, you turned lemons into lemonade.

As you probably know, volunteering opportunities arise almost daily. In any company in any job, tasks that no one wants to do will emerge. It may be that these tasks require a significant time commitment, have a slim chance of success, or are simply boring. Whatever the reason, everyone else avoids them.

You shouldn't. Volunteer consistently for these types of tasks and your boss will take notice. You'll develop a reputation for being proactive and committed, and this reputation will serve you well at promotion and bonus times.

5. DON'T MAKE EXCUSES, EVEN IF THEY HAVE SOME VALIDITY.

In school you may have relied on excuses ranging from "I was sick the day we covered that" to "The dog ate my homework" when you failed to turn in a paper or did poorly on a test. Taking responsibility means avoiding excuses whenever possible. Your customer doesn't care that his shipment was late because the truck broke down; your boss isn't interested in hearing how you missed the deadline because one of your team members didn't pull his weight. Responsible people swallow hard and stop themselves from rationalizing failure, and they do so consistently.

When I first joined Eicoff, my primary task was to generate new business for the agency. During that first year it was a struggle. I was only twenty-seven, the agency was not as well known as other agencies, people didn't return my calls, and the economy wasn't great. Al would stop by my office routinely and ask, "Get any new business today?" I hated to tell him no. I hated the disappointed, impatient look I received. I had plenty of excuses for why I was not getting any new business, but I resisted using them. Instead I would tell Al, "I'm working on it," and if I had talked to a prospective client that seemed interested, I would add, "I'm getting close." But I never misled him or painted a falsely rosy picture. He trusted me with the agency's future, and telling him that things were going great and I was going to land a number of big clients soon would have been a betrayal of that trust. Even though I believed I would land those clients, I didn't have any concrete evidence to offer, so I didn't tell him what I'm sure he wanted to hear.

Remind yourself that people who use excuses are essentially admitting that external forces are stronger than their internal will. They are saying, "I failed because of X, Y, and Z." Unconsciously they are looking for reasons to fail. Instead, look for ways to succeed, for fulfilling whatever responsibility you've taken on. As soon as you start spending too much time thinking about how you can explain or excuse your failure to your boss, you've lost.

Remind yourself, too, that some people take responsibility only with caveats and conditions. In other words, they say, "I'll do it, but if it doesn't work out, it will be X's fault." Or they will take on a time-consuming project but insist that if they do it effectively they should receive something in return (such as a raise, a bonus, a better office, better assignments). Caveats and conditions dilute your reputation for responsibility. Take on responsibility with no strings attached.

A WORD ABOUT IRRESPONSIBLE PEOPLE WHO SUCCEED

At this point, you may think about the people you work with and wonder how some of the irresponsible individuals there have done so well. You may know a senior vice president whom you regard as lazy, who has never taken on a tough or challenging assignment that wasn't forced upon him. You may be aware of another top executive who is brilliant at making excuses and keeping himself untainted by failure.

Don't believe for a moment that you can get away with this type of behavior. It inevitably will come back to haunt you. Yes, some irresponsible people do well in business. Sometimes their success is due to the highly political nature of their companies— gamesmanship is the primary competency in these cultures. Fortunately, the majority of companies aren't political hotbeds. They may be political, but not to the point that the most successful employees are those who are experts at manipulation. Most savvy leaders can quickly spot brownnosers and connivers and don't want them on their teams.

It is also true that people with great skills and expertise can become so valuable that they don't need to act responsibly. For example, the quintessential A student may believe herself so smart and competent that she's going to do well just about anywhere, even if she is lazy and rarely does something because it's the right thing to do.

Tell yourself that you're not this A student. You are more likely to be rewarded for who you are rather than how well you apply your knowledge to the job. I'm not suggesting that you're incompetent, only that you're going to be judged on broader criteria than your competencies.

Finally, you may know some top executive in your organization who acted irresponsibly in some way but seems to have gotten away with it. As a result, you may tell yourself that you, too, can get away with fabricating a credible excuse for why a project came up short or refusing to volunteer for a task that needed doing but would have taken up a lot of your time.

Don't fool yourself into believing any of this. Don't rationalize your irresponsible behavior by telling yourself that you only acted this way once or twice or that you can join another organization and start with a clean slate. Your behavior will catch up to you. If you act irresponsibly once and suffer no negative consequences, you will probably do it again. Eventually, your behavior will form a pattern that defines how you behave in work situations. Recall the blank piece of paper I discussed in the previous chapter and how you determine what words are written on it about you. Eventually, "irresponsible" will make it onto that list. Even if you leave the company and join a new one, your behavioral pattern will assert itself. You may have a clean slate when you first join the new company, but you're likely to revert to form and act irresponsibly over a period of time.

Gil, for instance, had charm to burn, and he often used it to escape unpleasant tasks and convince others to help him with jobs that he should have been doing on his own. A former athlete, handsome, and glib, Gil received a series of promotions early in his career. He started as a salesperson for a large corporation and did well, quickly moved to another organization of equal size, and within five years had received two promotions. His superiors knew that Gil manipulated others and found ways to avoid tasks he didn't like, and they had talked to him about this shortcoming. To Gil's credit, he tried to address these issues. After a few months of trying, however, he fell back into his old patterns.

A managerial opening came up in the company's hottest division—several senior executives had held this position, and it was considered a stepping-stone to the management ranks. Gil openly campaigned for the job and was convinced he would get it, since the only other person he was competing with was Nancy, whom Gil saw as a "plodder." While it was true that Nancy didn't have Gil's charm, she inspired much more trust and respect in the people who worked for her than Gil did. She never blamed others when a project she was involved with didn't succeed, accepting responsibility for whatever went wrong.

Nancy received the promotion, and when Gil heard that he hadn't been chosen, he went into his boss's office and protested that one of the job's requirements was wining and dining their top customers. "Nancy isn't half as good as I am at showing clients a good time," Gil said.

His boss replied, "She may not be half as good at showing them a good time, but she's more than twice as good at showing how committed she is to meeting their needs."

Convince yourself that you don't want to follow in the path of a successful but irresponsible individual you know by asking yourself the following questions:

- How would I feel if my child were to act the way this person acts at work?

- Would I hire this individual if I had my own business? Would I feel comfortable giving him important assignments that had a significant impact on the business?

- Do I feel that his expertise is more important than his character? If I had to make a choice, would I rather have someone working for me who was highly skillful or highly dependable?

- How many different ways can you think of that this person might cause problems? Might she prompt others to resent her because she slacks off and always blames others? Might this individual bring her boss or team down by not pulling her weight on projects that she's not particularly interested in?

THE BENEFITS OF BEING THE GO-TO GUY OR GAL

Taking responsibility seriously does more than make you an upstanding corporate citizen. Most large organizations have a list of leadership competencies for top positions, and seriously responsible people possess the qualities most companies are searching for. The responsible leader is great at getting things done, at meeting tough deadlines, at delivering what she promises. "Leadership maturity" has become an increasingly common buzzword in corporate circles because companies are looking for individuals who possess the traits that maturity connotes, and taking responsibility seriously is one critical aspect of maturity. Thus, people who take responsibility seriously early on are likely have a better shot at leadership roles than those who don't.

Given this, there are some specific ways seriously responsible C students benefit:

1. THEY RECEIVE THE BEST ASSIGNMENTS.

When you volunteer to do whatever needs to be done— including the worst jobs—eventually you also tend to get the best ones. When an important, challenging assignment arises, your boss doesn't want someone on it who might slack off or become discouraged. She wants someone she can depend on, and if you develop a reputation for responsibility, you're the one who will come to mind when making assignments. Obviously, working on the best projects puts your work in the spotlight and increases the chance that you'll get noticed . . . and promoted.

2. THEY GET PICKED FOR TEAMS THAT C STUDENTS ARE ROUTINELY EXCLUDED FROM.

In most organizations, various elite teams and task forces are formed to address critical organizational issues. A students, by virtue of their fast-track status, are often included on these teams. Developing a reputation for dependability and diligence will often qualify C students for membership in these elite groups. Team managers know they need a balance between people who are idea-generators and those who can execute; people who take responsibility seriously fall in this second category.

3. THEY WIN TIEBREAKERS WHEN BEING CONSIDERED FOR PROMOTIONS WITH OTHER CANDIDATES.

When it comes down to a race between candidates with roughly equal credentials, the one who is the more dependable usually wins. As much as managers respect skill and knowledge, they respect serious, responsible people even more. No one wants to be the one to promote someone who later turns out to be a problem, who ducks out of assignments, or fails to follow through on promises and disappoints high-level executives.

4. THEY BECOME STRONGER CANDIDATES FOR LEADERSHIP POSITIONS.

A board of directors wants a CEO who is hardworking, dependable, and doesn't make excuses, especially in today's climate where fiscally irresponsible CEOs have done terrible damage to their organizations. This requirement for the CEO position filters down to other leadership roles. Taking responsibility seriously doesn't mean you'll get one of these top jobs, but it certainly qualifies you for them.

WORDS OF WISDOM FROM A CONSISTENTLY RESPONSIBLE CEO

While almost all the people I interviewed for this book stressed how taking responsibility has helped their careers, Dennis Bookshester was especially emphatic about the role it played in his rise to CEO of retailer Carson Pirie Scott. At seventeen and a pre-med college student, Dennis's father died, and Dennis suddenly became responsible for taking care of his family. He dropped out of school and entered an executive training program, starting as a shoe salesman at Federated Department Stores (Burdines) and relatively quickly becoming head of merchandising. He moved on to Associated Dry Goods (Sibley's), where he had his first CEO position and orchestrated one of the first department store mergers. Based on his success at Associated, he was brought in at Carson's and had even greater success as their CEO. Later on Dennis also served as CEO of Fruit of the Loom, Zale's, and Turtle Wax. Dennis talked to me about how the sense of responsibility that was instilled in him after his father's death facilitated his business success.

"All of a sudden I was in charge. My mom and my sisters were depending on me. This gave me a subconscious sense of responsibility. It really wasn't something I thought about, but it became a big part of who I am. I always try to take charge.

"As time went on at Burdines, in order to grow I had to take on more and more responsibility. I couldn't say no—I almost had to overload myself. As my responsibility grew, I had to have the right people working with me and be a good teacher, teaching them what they had to accomplish. Doing this allowed me to take on even more responsibility. It just grew exponentially until I was running the whole merchandising function.

"I was always looking for more responsibility. I wasn't good at politics or schmoozing, but I was good at showing results and letting them speak for me. Whenever there were opportunities, I always threw my hat in the ring. I never thought about whether I had enough time or if I could really do something. I just did it."

I know that Dennis has achieved great success for other reasons—his retailing acumen, his ability to delegate and motivate—but Dennis's words paint a picture of an executive who prizes responsibility above all else. People like Dennis are immediately noticed and separate themselves from the crowd. Even at a young age they seem older than their years—they possess the maturity I referred to earlier. They earn respect not just for delivering results, but for their determination to deliver results.

This is an important distinction, especially early in a career. You will probably find yourself doing a lot of grunt work when you're relatively young and inexperienced, and you may not have a chance to show what you can do; you're going to be laboring in relative obscurity. While you may not be able to distinguish yourself on high-visibility projects, you can establish your reputation by how you handle the low-visibility ones. By demonstrating that you will work to the best of your ability no matter what the assignment and that you won't offer excuses if problems arise, you create a reputation as a solid, dependable employee. Because of this reputation, your bosses will give you an increased amount of responsibility—as Dennis describes it, your responsibility will grow exponentially. The more projects you take on, the more you demonstrate that you can be depended on to come through in a clutch, and the more future important assignments you'll receive.

People talk about the mystique or aura of highly charismatic individuals. I believe that highly responsible people also possess this mystique. When you meet someone like Dennis, you immediately feel that you're in the presence of someone who will do whatever it takes to get the job done. You have absolute confidence in his ability to step up, take charge, and be personally accountable for whatever task you set before him.

Just about everyone has the capability to project this aura. Let's explore what you can do to develop it.

HOW TO BUILD A SERIOUSLY RESPONSIBLE IMAGE

Be aware that responsibility and irresponsibility are not either/or choices. There is a gray area between the two extremes that many highly competent executives occupy. Some people are responsible, but they take their responsibility lightly. In other words, they accept that they should be diligent and dutiful, but they don't give it much thought or feel it's particularly important. There is an opportunity for C students to compete in this gray area. They may have taken their responsibilities lightly in the past, not realizing that making a greater effort could pay dividends for their careers. They must recognize that if they want to get ahead, they should do more than others; that through their persistence and almost obsessive desire to do the best job they can, they will earn recognition. To them, responsibility isn't just a word but a religion. They believe fervently in their responsibilities.

To communicate this belief, you should take the following five steps:

1. RECOGNIZE AND GO AFTER THE LATRINE-CLEANING JOBS.

There are jobs in every company that everyone avoids because they are tedious and time-consuming. Generally a manager assigns these tasks because no one volunteers for them. When people are forced to do them, they generally do them sloppily. Break the pattern by raising your hand, taking on these grunt jobs, and doing them as well as you possibly can. Yes, they're boring and it's difficult to feign excitement about an inherently tedious task. At the same time, you can view the task as a means to an end. It is a kind of test: If you can do a good job with the small stuff, bosses will feel more comfortable entrusting you with bigger responsibilities. Hank Johnson, former CEO of Spiegel and the man responsible for the company's dramatic turnaround in the 1970s, wrote an autobiography, *The Corporate Dream,* in which he talked about one of his first jobs, and how he was assigned to sweep the floor. He vowed to himself that he would do this menial task better than anyone who ever had the position before, convinced that if he showed himself to be a responsible floor sweeper he would be given assignments in which he could better display his expertise.

2. RECOGNIZE AND GO AFTER THE HIGH-DEGREE-OF-DIFFICULTY JOBS.

After you gain a certain amount of experience, you're ready to volunteer for more challenging jobs. These jobs, too, are avoided by most people because they are difficult and the likelihood of failure is high. As I noted before, though, even if you fail you will have demonstrated your willingness to take responsibility for a tough job, and if you succeed you're a hero. Don't be intimidated by what your colleagues tell you, since some of them certainly will imply that you'd have to be nuts to take on a given assignment or that only a masochist would volunteer for project X. What they are really saying is that they lack the diligence and problem-solving skills to handle these high-degree-of-difficulty jobs effectively. Keep tackling these tough assignments and don't be discouraged by failure. People will recognize your courage, a key trait of anyone who takes responsibility seriously.

3. BE CONSCIOUS OF YOUR IMPULSE TO BLAME, COMPLAIN, AND OFFER EXCUSES . . . AND STIFLE THIS IMPULSE.

Taking full responsibility for your actions and those of anyone who works with and for you means no blaming, complaining, or excuse-making. This is easier said than done, of course, because a colleague's or direct report's mistake may cause you to miss a deadline you promised you'd meet. It's human nature to want to tell your boss that you would have met that deadline if not for John's mistake. If you make this excuse, though, you're communicating that you don't want to be responsible, and this will reflect poorly on you.

Remind yourself continuously not to give in to the "It's not my fault" impulse. It may not be your fault in one sense, but if you took responsibility for the outcome of a task or project, you should have anticipated that John might be too busy with other tasks and was likely to make a mistake. While you might want to talk to John privately about what he did wrong, your public stance should be that it's your fault and that you'll accept the consequences. Even if those consequences are significant—removal from a team, a demotion— accept them graciously. While your boss or some other executive may be disappointed in you, other organization leaders will respect the way you handled yourself and will remember it the next time a key project comes along or a position opens up.

4. DON'T LET FEAR GET IN THE WAY OF TAKING RESPONSIBILITY SERIOUSLY.

I'm not going to pretend that taking responsibility seriously is easy. In some situations it can be frightening. When a lot is riding on the outcome of a project or initiative for which you're responsible, you're naturally going to be anxious. You may find yourself in a position where you or others will lose their jobs if you don't meet your goal. Your boss may be counting on you to deliver and she may put a lot of pressure on you to come through for her. The relationship with a customer or a client may depend on you doing a good job. Taking on these heavy responsibilities is scary, but fear, if you let it, will cause you to act in cowardly or unethical ways.

One day shortly after I joined Eicoff, I was walking down the hallway and noticed that Nancy, a media buyer, was crying. I asked her what was wrong, and she told me that one of our clients, the CEO of the company, had been yelling at her for a minor error. As Nancy explained what happened, it became clear that the client was being a bully. I didn't even consider talking to Alvin about the incident and having him deal with the client, whom he knew well. Though I didn't relish the confrontation with this CEO, who could be very intimidating, I felt it was my responsibility as a senior executive to deal with it directly. I called him and said, "You can't treat our people this way."

He responded, "I'll treat them any way I want."

"If you continue to treat them this way, you'll be looking for another agency."

Fortunately, this CEO was very savvy and recognized the value the agency provided his company. Still, we could have lost the account, and it would have been a serious loss at that time. I would have had the dubious distinction of having lost a client before bringing one into the agency. This was a scary thought, but my greater responsibility was to Nancy, and so I did what I had to do. It's worth noting that the agency still has this client.

About twelve years later, after having just been appointed CEO, I found myself in a similar situation. I was holding my second staff meeting with the agency's officers, and during the meeting one of our executives made a mildly negative remark about another executive who was not in attendance. A third executive, whom I'll refer to as Gordon, threw a fit. He shouted, "I won't stand for this [the negative comment about the absent executive]! I won't be a part of this organization!" Gordon, you must understand, was very smart. His outburst was calculated to challenge my authority. Not only was he older than me and resentful that Alvin had named me CEO, but his accounts generated a significant percentage of Eicoff's total revenue.

As Gordon started to walk out of the room and approached the door, I said, "Gordon, if you walk out of the agency tonight, you don't work here anymore."

My heart was pounding so loudly I thought everyone in the room could hear it. As Gordon continued walking through the door and out of sight, I could not believe what I had just done. Gordon could take millions of dollars in revenue away from the agency. In my first few months as CEO, I would have managed to lose an enormous amount of billings.

I was relieved, then, when Gordon reentered the conference room a few seconds later and said, "Oh, I left my glasses." Rather than pick up his glasses and depart again, he sat down and remained with the agency.

As CEO, I was responsible for the agency's culture. I wanted to establish an environment free from the grandstanding and game playing that Gordon favored. Though I was afraid of losing all the business he controlled, I knew my responsibility for the culture superseded this fear. As scary as it was, this incident was a turning point in my career. In that moment, I established my authority and made it clear that I would not tolerate such behavior. I gained respect from everyone in that room because I took my responsibility as CEO seriously.

5. EXPAND YOUR AREA OF RESPONSIBILITY FROM WHAT YOU HAVE TO DO TO WHAT NEEDS TO BE DONE.

This is another important distinction. Everyone has assigned areas of responsibility. Your job defines the tasks you need to accomplish and the limits of your authority. While it makes no sense to ignore these boundaries routinely—to do so would result in chaos—opportunities arise when you need to step over them and act in the organization's best interest. Every employee is responsible for helping the company achieve key business goals, and if you have an idea that will help the company meet a business objective, you should consider acting on it.

For instance, Heather Lang is an Eicoff media supervisor on the Liberty Medical account. One of Liberty Medical's products involves a service for people with diabetes, and we were in the process of looking for a celebrity spokesperson as part of a change in strategy. The commercial we had previously created wasn't beating the control, and trying to make it work was frustrating. Our creative people were searching for a celebrity with diabetes to serve as spokesperson, but unfortunately they weren't finding anyone who fit our requirements in terms of image, age, and other factors.

Even though it was clearly a creative rather than a media responsibility, Heather saw that the creative department wasn't having much luck, so she did her own research. After a great deal of effort she discovered that Wilford Brimley was a diabetic. His avuncular style, age, and believability made him the perfect spokesperson, and he has helped Liberty Medical grow tremendously.

NOT EVERYONE IS CREATED EQUALLY RESPONSIBLE

It stands to reason that some of you are naturally or situationally more responsible than others. It may be that you were the older sibling in your family and consequently had more responsibility thrust upon you from an early age. It may also be that, like Dennis Bookshester, your family situation forced you to become more responsible at an earlier age than most people. And it may be that your corporate culture emphasizes responsibility, and this culture has accelerated your growth as a person and as an employee.

No matter where you are on the responsibility continuum, though, taking responsibility seriously is a matter of awareness and effort. Even if you're naturally responsible, you can still act irresponsibly in work situations—you can convince yourself that the people who play politics are the ones who get ahead, and you can go against your nature and blame others when things go off course. Consistently making yourself conscious about the need to be responsible and expending the effort that responsibility requires, therefore, are mandatory for all C students. It is something you can do no matter where you come from, how many false starts you've made in your career, or even if you don't have an off-the-charts IQ. Everyone has the capability of taking responsibility seriously, but C students need to be more motivated than A students to capitalize on this capability. Sooner or later, most C students recognize that if they're going to get ahead, they need to give themselves an edge— and a reputation for being responsible can serve as that edge.

In advertising we talk a great deal about branding products and services. In any career, you need to create a brand for yourself that includes the qualities discussed throughout this book. And taking responsibility seriously should be at the top of the list. As quality is to a product's brand, responsibility is to a C student's career. Everything you do at work—from the way you answer the phone and return calls promptly to your willingness to work extra hours to meet important deadlines—contributes to your particular brand. If you do all these things in a responsible manner, you'll find that you will become a very marketable brand.

CHAPTER 5

MASTER THE ART OF
PURPOSEFUL LEARNING

Many of you may not have been considered great learners by the school system, but you can become great learners in the real world. Flip Filipowski, Art Frigo, Dennis Bookshester, Rich Melman, Mike Waters, and many of the other high achievers I've interviewed all spoke of their ability to learn on the job and how this ability has helped them succeed. This learning doesn't involve sitting at a desk, taking notes, and spitting back what a boss wants to hear. Instead, the purposeful learning referred to in this chapter's title is all about observation.

Focused observation. Constant observation. Open-minded observation. Some people may learn on the job in spite of themselves. They keep their minds closed to learning unless their boss says to them something along the lines of, "Listen up—this is how you do this task." Other people restrict their learning because of their superior attitudes. They are afraid to let anyone see that they don't know something, so they refuse to ask questions or request assistance. Still others just aren't paying attention or remove themselves from learning environments—you'll recall my story about Mike, a colleague early in my career who stayed in his office by himself as much as possible.

You need to observe more than the facts. Knowing how to do the basic tasks of your job is important, but you also need to know how to project an air of confidence and competence, how to carry yourself when you walk into a room, how to deal with difficult but important people, how to lead during a crisis, and how to adapt to changing circumstances. Flip Filipowski refers to all these types of knowledge as "diversified learning," and that's a great way to describe what the best observers acquire. To help you acquire diversified learning, let's start out with how you can learn from an amazing range of people and situations.

EVERYONE AND EVERY EXPERIENCE IS A POTENTIAL TEACHER: KEEPING YOUR EYES, EARS, AND MIND OPEN

Earlier, I told you the story of one of my grandfathers and the lesson he taught me about the importance of reputation. Now I'd like to share a story about my other grandfather, a street junk peddler. He would buy just about anything from anyone—bathtubs, copper wire, and everything in between. One day when I was twelve or so, he said, "We're going to be partners for a week."

"What does that mean, Zaydie?" I asked him.

"I'm going to teach you to do what I do."

He bought junk from various places, and that day he took me to a garbage dump in Aliquippa, Pennsylvania, at precisely 12:30 in the afternoon, when the guys who worked on the city garbage trucks would gather. They had selected particular items they perceived as having value that were being thrown out and placed them in piles for my grandfather's inspection. Before we approached them, my grandfather pointed out each of his customers and gave me advice about how to deal with them.

"This guy, you don't have to negotiate. He'll take whatever you offer, so be fair. This guy over there, he loves to negotiate, so he'll start high and you start low, but don't worry, he loves the process and you'll end up in the middle. Over there, that one," he said, pointing, "he is never happy with the deal, so you may have to walk away from the sale. And that guy, you have to laugh with him."

My grandfather had never read anything about customer sales or taken a course in the subject, but he instinctively knew how to negotiate. Despite his appearance and rough edges, he understood that you had to know your customer, and that you had to treat different customers differently. It was a great lesson to learn early on, and I've applied it throughout my career.

I'm not sure if software entrepreneur Flip Filipowski learned any lessons from his grandparents, but I do know that he is extremely open to a wide range of knowledge sources. He is not one of those high-tech people who is only interested in what takes place on a computer screen. A voracious reader and a keen observer of life, Flip believes that it is the synergy between one area of knowledge and a very different area that produces great business ideas. As he says, "If you stick with what you know and do it well, eventually you'll stagnate and become someone who repeats tasks, growing tired and old in the process. As opposed to someone who transfers learning from one area to another and ends up crossing a boundary no one has ever crossed before. Maybe you've learned a lot about koi and carp production and you already know a great deal about building automobiles, and the synergy between these two areas produces something that's innovative. It's really nothing more than a transference of knowledge, but this coming together of two seemingly unrelated ideas is the source of many great entrepreneurial successes."

Being open to learning means more than just acquiring more knowledge about a given subject. It also involves picking up cues about behavior and attitude that can affect how others in an organization perceive you. Bill McCabe, an Eicoff senior vice president, helped his career when he was a young executive by paying attention to how other people dressed. When Bill started out, he didn't realize that he dressed like someone who would never make it out of the middle-management ranks. He had to develop his sense of style, and to help him do this I used to take him for walks down Michigan Avenue. When someone who looked like a businessman would approach us, I would say to Bill, "upper management" or "middle management." I helped him realize that the choice of a certain color or brand or type of suit communicated something about an individual. Some people dressed indifferently and looked unprofessional. Some people took great care in their choice of a wardrobe and seemed to have a spark others lacked. I'm not endorsing the old cliché that clothes make the man, but I do believe that they help bring out who that man is. Bill began to pay attention not only to how people dressed but how they carried themselves in different situations, and he was able to use this learning to craft his own effective image.

There are many unorthodox areas of learning, but the following four are easy to focus on and may help you achieve career goals that more traditional learning couldn't help you achieve:

1. LESSONS FROM FAMILY ELDERS.

A surprisingly large number of the people interviewed referred to a piece of advice from parents or grandparents that helped them succeed. It may not have been a specific career tip. Instead it may have been value gleaned through observing that person's behavior over time. Or it may have involved a specific incident that

made an impression when the individual was young. Not everyone, though, recognizes that lessons taught by elders within a
family setting can apply to business and careers. In most cultures,
older members of the tribe are considered to possess wisdom because of their accumulated experiences and the perspective provided by age. In our culture, we often ignore this wisdom. The odds
are that some older member of your family has told you a story or
shared a lesson that you might not have taken to heart. I would
advise you to think back and give serious consideration to something a parent or grandparent communicated to you, and to reflect on how it might apply to whatever job or career challenge
you're currently facing.

2. OPPORTUNITIES TO ACQUIRE KNOWLEDGE THAT HAVE NOTHING TO DO WITH YOUR JOB.

I am a student of history; Art Frigo is an expert in subjects as
diverse as car racing and olive oil. In fact, many high achievers are
avid readers and world travelers and have hobbies they're passionate about. In other words, they relish opportunities to acquire
knowledge about subjects that have no direct bearing on their
professions. Indirectly, though, this knowledge provides them
with perspective and helps them become well rounded in ways
some of the brightest people aren't. While specialists may be brilliant in one area, they often lack the ability to carry on conversations with people who aren't interested in their particular area of
expertise. People who are eager to learn about a lot of things usually can use what they learn in work situations. If they are managers or in leadership roles, they need to be able to relate to and
motivate people from all types of backgrounds, and a well-rounded
person is able to do this far better than a specialist. I'm not sure if
my knowledge of history has helped me craft better advertising

strategies for my clients, but I suspect that I have unconsciously applied some historical lessons in my work situations.

3. WORK SUBJECTS THAT SEEM OUTSIDE OF YOUR AREA OF INTEREST.

At the start of my career I was convinced that I wanted to produce commercials. I had taken advertising courses in college and was certain that I would enjoy the process of creating television commercials. It was a ridiculous idea, since I have the patience of a gnat. Still, at the time it made sense to me, and when I first joined an ad agency as an account executive my goal was to transfer to a creative job. When I attended my first shoot, though, the experience was like watching paint dry. I could no more spend hours trying to get the lighting right for a scene than I could pilot the space shuttle. Fortunately, I was open to learning other aspects of the ad business, and I discovered that what I really liked was developing relationships with clients. At first learning how to develop these relationships seemed outside my stated goal of producing commercials, but I gradually realized that this new area of knowledge would help me succeed in advertising.

4. PERSONAL STYLES.

This one is simple. Pay attention to how people you respect and admire present themselves. Note their clothes, their speaking habits, and how their offices appear. You don't need to copy any one individual, but you can pick up valuable tips that will help you to be conscious about the image you're presenting and what that says about you as an employee, a manager, and a leader.

THE TRICKS OF THE TRADE: PAY ATTENTION TO THE SUBTLE AND NOT-SO-SUBTLE WAYS PEOPLE GET THINGS DONE

No matter what organization you work for or what field you're in, you will have colleagues and bosses who have developed techniques that aren't found in any textbook. They have crafted their own methods and approaches for solving problems, cutting through red tape, and resolving conflicts. As a C student, you may not have done so well in problem-solving and conflict-resolution courses, but the real test is how well you absorb related lessons in the workplace.

When I joined Eicoff, my mission was to generate new business. Unfortunately, I knew next to nothing about selling. I had to learn fast, and the teacher available to me was Al Eicoff. I wasn't under any illusion that I was going to be able to copy his selling approach. He possessed an in-your-face style, favoring bluster and blarney over making logical arguments. This didn't fit with my personality, and I knew I couldn't sell exactly as Al did. Nonetheless, I paid attention to his approach, and I observed that at times Al would stop talking and listen hard to what a client or prospective client was saying. Clients seemed to come alive when they were given the chance to present their particular problem or goal, and they seemed pleased with Al's response if he merely nodded his head while they talked.

Over time, I adopted this listening technique. When meeting with a potential client I would try to let them speak first rather than launch into a prepared presentation. This way, I could determine what they were really concerned about and what they really wanted from an agency. I would then adapt my presentation to these concerns, and it would help demonstrate that I was on their wavelength.

When Eicoff became a division of Ogilvy, I paid attention to how Ogilvy executives got things done. I admired their professionalism and their ability to attract and keep top corporate clients, and I knew that if Eicoff was going to flourish as part of the Ogilvy network, I would have to learn how they conducted business and transfer some of their style and substance to the Eicoff culture. After years as a smaller, independent agency, the Eicoff philosophy was to shoot from the hip. This worked fine with entrepreneurial clients, but it became clear that this would not work during joint presentations with Ogilvy or with some of the more buttoned-down Fortune 500 clients we hoped to land. At first, trying to learn how they did business was a challenge. When they talked about "decks" (printed transcripts of a slide presentation), I had no idea what they were referring to. After observing and asking questions when necessary, though, I began to see the way they planned for a meeting, used a variety of sophisticated tools during presentations, and even why and when they took their clients to certain restaurants. Though some of their approach was not compatible with the Eicoff culture and I had no intention of changing Eicoff's to our detriment, I was able to integrate certain methods into the Eicoff approach, especially when it came to working with large corporate clients.

When it comes to learning the tricks of the trade, though, Senator Howard Carroll has few peers. As I've emphasized, he figured out the world of politics—where there are even more tricks to learn than in business—by absorbing every lesson the late Mayor Daley imparted. One particular lesson came early on in his career when he was in law school with the mayor's son (and now the current mayor of Chicago), who he refers to as Ritchie. Howie and Ritchie were partners in a law school moot court competition, and they were working extremely hard to win. Many times, they would study together at Mayor Daley's home, and the mayor noticed that the many hours they were putting into this effort were taking away from the time they needed to put into their other courses. At one point the mayor took Howie aside and asked him to explain the legal issue that they were working on, a complex aviation case. Howie did so, and then the mayor asked, "How much time are you putting into it?"

"A lot," Howie said.

"Are you graded on how you do?"

"No, it's pass/fail."

"Well, let me ask you this," the mayor said. "Do you want to win the nationals? How much does it matter if you only do okay, but still pass?"

"That would be fine."

"Maybe there are other things you might be spending your time on?"

In hindsight, Howie realized that the mayor had taught him two key lessons, which he later used in politics. First, he learned that while some things may seem more important than others in the heat of the moment, you have to step back and evaluate what your real priorities are. Years later, as an officeholder besieged with requests for his time and assistance, Howie realized how critical prioritizing was for success in politics. Second, and perhaps less obviously, he grasped that the mayor had led him to this first realization not by delivering a lecture or telling him what to do, but by asking questions and letting him discover the answers for himself. This indirect way of getting people to do the right thing has come in handy in politics.

The story, though, doesn't end there. To Howie's surprise, the mayor began talking with great knowledge about the legal ramifications of the case he and Ritchie were working on, and Howie asked, "With all due respect, Mr. Mayor, you haven't practiced law for years. How would you know about this aviation issue?"

The mayor, with a twinkle in his eye, said, "United Airlines. O'Hare Airport. They are in Chicago."

The third trick of the trade Howie gleaned was that you had better know about everything that takes place under your watch, and know it better than anyone might expect you to know it.

Finally, the day arrived and Howie and Ritchie were going to present in moot court. A judge, a professor, and a lawyer were going to hear their case, but heeding the mayor's advice, they wanted to pass but lose. By losing they wouldn't have to remain in the competition and do even more work in preparation for the next round. With the instinct of a born politician, Howie knew he had little influence over the professor's vote, but he figured he might be able to do something with the lawyer and the judge. So before the moot court class began, he talked to each of them. First, he met with the judge and related his discussion with the mayor and how it might be best if they pass but lose. Next, he had a similar conversation with the lawyer, who surprised Howie by saying that their opponent in the moot court case was the lawyer's cousin—and this cousin had already spoken to the lawyer and requested that they pass but lose. The lawyer added that his cousin's aunt had also talked to him and insisted that her child lose.

Howie then said, "Well, I guess it's a choice between family and career."

Howie and Richie lost the competition by a 2 to 1 vote. Perhaps more important, though, Howie realized that in politics, it's often who you know that counts more than what you know.

Norm Bobins, president and CEO of Chicago's LaSalle Bank, has a much shorter story about learning the tricks of the trade, but one that's equally apt. Early in his career, Norm worked at American National Bank, whose president at the time was Alan Stultz. A self-made man who started out as a messenger at the Federal Reserve and never went to college, Stultz emphasized to Norm that he should learn from life experiences, not just from the conventional wisdom of banking. At the time, a great deal of importance was placed on long-term planning. Stultz, though, told Norm, "Long-term planning is wonderful, but if you keep your eye on ninety days, you can't go wrong."

"He would focus on what we could do better right at this moment and always ask how are we doing now. It was a very good lesson to learn," Norm says.

Whether you're in banking, politics, law, business, or any profession, you need to master two levels of knowledge. The first may be taught in school and involves the processes and procedures, techniques and tools that are codified and found in books and professors' lectures. The second type of knowledge is tacit; it exists in the minds of practitioners who have developed their particular know-how through years of experience. The only way you're going to acquire this knowledge is by closely observing how these savvy individuals act in different situations.

The lesson is, don't assume you know everything because you studied it in school or attended company training workshops. To learn the tricks of the trade, you have to watch the experts, see how they behave, and hope they will be generous and share their tactics with you.

LEARN WHAT NOT TO DO

Most people learn naturally from positive experiences. Learning from a boss or human resources trainer is not so different from absorbing lessons from a teacher. At work, your boss or someone else in authority provides information and ideas, and you integrate what you learn into your job performance. C students, however, need to go beyond this positive learning model and take advantage of negative learning. This is another way they can gain a competitive edge. Fortunately, many C students are accustomed to learning from negative events. After all, most C students know what it's like to blow an exam or turn in an assignment late. They learn the hard way that certain behaviors are counterproductive and some situations cause them trouble. They understand that by learning what not to do, they can increase their odds of succeeding.

My daughter, Debbie, was a successful ad agency executive, but after some early positive jobs she found herself working for a boss she hated. This boss was mean-spirited, short-sighted, and devious, and my daughter clearly thought that there was nothing to be gained from the experience. When Debbie told me about the situation, I said, "You know, you've worked for some wonderful people in the past, and you've learned great leadership skills from them. Here's a situation that's terrible, your boss is making you miserable. But you know what: You can learn as much or more from this experience as all the positive ones. What you can learn is what not to do."

Most people enter the business world without a clear idea of what type of leader or manager or boss they should be. After a while, though, they gain a sense of what qualities they admire and want to emulate. It's just as important, though, to know which qualities to avoid because they make leaders less effective than they might otherwise be. It sometimes takes seeing a bullying boss in action before you can learn to manage your own bullying tendencies. It may be that you have a boss who is smart and accomplished but a terrible communicator, and you realize that all the wisdom you possess doesn't do much good unless you make an effort to communicate it clearly. Obviously, it's no fun to work for someone you dislike, but it also can be an opportunity in disguise.

Janice, a highly successful consultant with her own firm, once worked for a consultant, Grant, who had a reputation as a brilliant strategist; he had been a professor at a top business school and was frequently quoted in *Fortune* and the *Wall Street Journal*. Grant hired Janice away from a good job at another consulting firm by telling her she would have a chance to become a partner faster working for him. What Grant didn't tell Janice was that he was an egotist who didn't like sharing the spotlight. Janice found that Grant tended to use his intellect to intimidate everyone he worked with, and his smarmy attitude with clients made his people despise his duplicity. Janice stayed at the consulting firm for two years, and though she didn't enjoy working with Grant she believes that her ultimate success as the head of her own firm was due in part to this experience.

"I, too, could easily have suffered from some of the same flaws as Grant," she said. "When you're a management consultant working with high-profile leaders and clients and you pull off a major deal or help implement a precedent-setting strategy, your ego becomes inflated. I learned from Grant how to manage my ego and present the same face to my direct reports as I do to my clients. Most of my people have been with me for more than five years, and in our business that kind of loyalty is rare. I attribute it to what I learned from Grant about how not to be a leader."

You can also learn which types of jobs and careers aren't right for you from negative situations. Art Frigo, for instance, didn't realize at the start of his career that he was a born entrepreneur. In fact, he worked for corporate giant 3M in sales, and though 3M was a great company and presented him with good opportunities, Art recognized that being a spoke in the corporate wheel was not for him. They wouldn't let him expand his area of expertise—at the time, he wanted to transfer to a corporate market planning position—but he also saw that his entrepreneurial instincts wouldn't flourish in this environment.

"No one could believe I left 3M when I did," Art said. "It turned out to be the right decision, but logic told me not to leave, since it was a great job with lots of opportunities. But I wanted to grow, and I wasn't growing there."

Becky Jewett, former president of catalog house Norm Thompson Outfitters, recalled how as a young woman she had been promoted to head of personnel, but her boss was not particularly enamored of women executives, especially ones without advanced degrees. As a result he paid Becky only $16,000, which was $8,000 less than anyone in that position had made before. When Becky protested, her boss said, "Honey, first of all, girls don't have to make decisions, and you don't want to have that type of role. And second, sweetie, why do you have to make $24,000?"

It was at that point that Becky saw the light and realized that to be viewed as a decision maker she needed to get an MBA, which is what she did.

The following is a list of common negative work and career situations. No doubt you've experienced some of them, and perhaps you haven't learned as much from them as you might have. Think about what you might learn the next time you find yourself in one of these situations:

- Working for a lousy boss

- Being fired

- Being part of a corporate culture with values you find offensive

- Having a good boss who micromanages the work he assigns

- Losing a major customer or client

- Being part of a team marked by conflict and an unwillingness to compromise

- Having a job that you find excruciatingly boring

- Working for someone who is highly skilled but unethical

- Finding that you're really good at your job but not challenged by it

LEARNING TO ADJUST

One of the truisms that apply to most C students is that their careers won't follow a straight line. Unlike someone who knows she wants to work for Procter & Gamble or IBM from the time she enters a top business school, most C students encounter roadblocks and detours on the way to finding their true calling. When those roadblocks and detours present themselves, you need to learn to adjust and reset your job and career aspirations. If you don't, you may end up wasting months or even years pursuing the wrong job or in the wrong field.

Earlier I mentioned how I learned to adjust to the fact that I was not cut out to be a television commercial producer. An even more difficult adjustment, though, took place a few years before that, when I was in college. Growing up, my dream was to become a professional baseball player. That was the image that I had for my future, and I had it listed in my high school yearbook as my goal. When I reached the University of Arizona and played on their team, though, I realized that I was just another fair-to-middling college player. It was terribly painful when I came to accept this fact, but I learned from it and adjusted my career goals and dreams. If I had not done so, I might have spent years hanging on with some low-level minor league team and delayed the start of my real career.

As the CEO of an ad agency, I have seen many people who refuse to learn from roadblocks and detours. There are very talented copywriters who dream of becoming creative directors, but their management and leadership skills don't match their writing skills. Nonetheless, they refuse to accept the reality of their situation and either keep beating their heads against the wall and trying to secure a creative director position or moving from one agency to the next in a futile search for such a job. I have also witnessed lawyers who dream of becoming a partner even when it's clear that their firms don't see them as partner material and life insurance agents who believe they will one day join the million-dollar roundtable but don't have a chance of reaching this level.

The problem is that few bosses are willing to level with people and say, "You're never going to realize your dream," or words to that effect. No one wants to be responsible for crushing another person's spirit, so they turn people down for jobs softly, saying, "I'm sorry, you didn't get it this time, but maybe next time you'll have better luck."

You need to read between the lines in situations like these and adjust accordingly. If you don't, you may become obsessed with getting a job or achieving a level of success that is clearly out of your reach. There are too many smart, talented people out there who instead of switching gears and finding what's right for them end up becoming bitter and frustrated at what they don't achieve.

I'm not a sailor, but from what I understand good sailors learn to make continuous adjustments based on shifts in wind speed and direction. Likewise, your career is going to encounter similar shifts. You can either fight these shifts or adjust to the situation. I have told you about Alvin Eicoff and my great fondness and respect for him, but toward the end of his career he tended to fight industry shifts. He didn't like the way the world was changing, and constantly brought up how he used to create highly effective commercials for $5,000. He resisted the idea of combining branding strategies with television direct-response advertising or testing commercials that were shorter than the standard 120-second direct-response length. Once, the agency created a commercial for Galderma Labs, and we showed it to Al when he returned from a vacation. The results from the spot had been terrific, and everyone was eager for Al to see the spot. After viewing it, though, Al said, "It's not the way I would have done it," and then walked out. Despite this dismissive behavior, Al never understood why people didn't come into his office and ask for his advice. He was so eager to share what he knew, but his refusal to adjust to change discouraged people from asking him for help.

Becky Jewett, on the other hand, was astute about adjusting based on fresh knowledge. After a series of successes, Becky was in great demand for top jobs at many companies. At one point she took a job with a major corporation, where she was well paid and had a great deal of responsibility. What she didn't have was a challenge.

She says, "What I learned about myself is that I'm really bad when I'm in bureaucratic situations and all I do is maintain the status quo. That drives me nuts; I get bored and sloppy. I would much rather be faced with challenging problems, have intellectual stimulation, and deal with growth opportunities."

For this reason, she left her bureaucratic position to become president of a smaller division within the corporation, and she found that position much more to her liking. Becky had learned that for her challenging positions were preferable to comfortable, stress-free ones.

To learn to adjust as Becky did means using your powers of observation to their fullest capacity. If you don't pay attention continuously and perceptively, you're going to miss the signals that tell you it's time to change course. With that in mind, I'll leave you with five tips on responding to situations where you may need to make adjustments.

1. BE ALERT FOR SITUATIONS IN WHICH YOU FEEL LIKE YOU'RE BEING STYMIED IN YOUR ATTEMPTS TO ACHIEVE CERTAIN GOALS OR OUTCOMES.

Are you constantly applying for and being turned down for a specific type of job? Do you have certain expectations of a job that aren't being met? Be aware that something is stopping you from moving forward, and that awareness should be a sign that you may have something to learn from this situation.

2. ASK SOMEONE YOU TRUST TO LEVEL WITH YOU ABOUT WHY YOU'RE BEING STYMIED.

As I noted, people are often reluctant to talk straight about why you're not moving forward. You need to confront someone— your boss, your boss's boss, a colleague—and demand to be told what the problem is. It may be that you've just been unlucky. It may also be that you're pursuing an unachievable goal.

3. FORCE YOURSELF NOT TO BE DEFENSIVE WHEN THIS INDIVIDUAL LEVELS WITH YOU.

You're not going to learn anything if you try to have a debate about why you really are leadership material or attack the other person for being honest. If you trust this person, you need to accept what she says without protest.

4. CONCENTRATE ON WHAT YOU CAN LEARN FROM THIS EXPERIENCE THAT WILL HELP YOUR CAREER RATHER THAN BEAT YOURSELF UP FOR YOUR INADEQUACIES.

Are you learning that you're not well-suited to a specific job, company, or profession? Are you discovering that you might do better in a different type of corporate culture or working for a different type of boss?

5. FIGURE OUT WHAT ADJUSTMENTS YOU MIGHT MAKE THAT WOULD INCREASE YOUR JOB EFFECTIVENESS OR IMPROVE YOUR CAREER PROSPECTS.

It may not require a major change such as leaving your company or your chosen field. It may simply mean you need to develop a skill you're lacking or become more open-minded about a particular issue. Sometimes a small change in how you act or think about a work issue can have a big impact on how you're perceived within an organization.

AN ASTONISHING ON-THE-JOB LEARNER IN A FIELD WHERE THERE'S A LOT TO LEARN

Few businesses are as difficult to master as the restaurant business, and few people in the history of the field have been as successful at it as Rich Melman. Lettuce Entertain You Enterprises (LEYE), Rich's restaurant empire, is legendary for the amazingly large number of hits it's had over the years and the amazingly low number of misses. LEYE's restaurants are known both for the high quality of their food and the originality of their concepts; they also have superb business plans. Given all this, you might think Rich was an MBA or at least had gone to a famous restaurant management school. In fact, he was an indifferent student who learned what he needed to know by observing and doing.

Rich is a great model for anyone who feels that they can't learn as fast or as well as others, based on their school experiences. He embodies the type of purposeful learning that I've been describing. As he says, "I have tunnel vision. When I'm focused on something, nothing else matters. If I concentrate on something, I can be good at it. But I'm a moron in other areas. When I was a kid, I was excellent at sports like baseball, but when it came to something like bowling, I was terrible. I didn't concentrate on it.

"Real smart people have an advantage in that they can be a doctor, a lawyer, an accountant. I didn't have that luxury. I tried to be a salesman at first and I was awful. I was a Fuller Brush salesman, and people slammed the door in my face. I wasn't good at asking for the sale. I learned I was better at doing favors for others rather than asking them to do something for me."

In other words, Rich learned what not to do by drawing a lesson from his failure, and he learned what to do through intense observation of something he loved.

CHAPTER 6

TAKE ADVANTAGE OF
UNEXPECTED OPPORTUNITIES

A students receive great grades in part because they capitalize on expected opportunities. In school, they are astute about what they must do to obtain top marks, and they do it. In their careers, many A students also make it their business to know what it takes to get ahead in a given company. For this reason, they often follow a relatively predictable path, receiving job offers and job assignments suited to the fast track. They assume they will be offered jobs by companies like General Electric and major consulting firms like McKinsey. They expect to be promoted to managerial positions after a short period of time as individual contributors. They are confident that they will receive partnership offers in professional service firms after putting in their years as associates. As long as they work hard and view their careers strategically, their opportunities will come to them.

C students, on the other hand, must be alert for unexpected opportunities. More than that, they have to put themselves in positions to seize these opportunities when they arise. As you probably have already learned, you aren't going to be the automatic choice for a top job or the person who is handed the most challenging, visible assignment. You may not be the one chosen for the executive training program. The good news is that you can create or seize unexpected chances to gain experience and shine. You can impress a boss, acquire a critical skill, or achieve a significant goal in all sorts of ways that other people in your organization may ignore. You shouldn't ignore them, so let's look at the range of unexpected opportunities available to you.

OVERLOOKED ASSIGNMENTS, JOBS, AND SITUATIONS THAT CAN OFFER A BIG BOOST TO YOUR CAREER

Think about some of the unexpected jobs and experiences of the high achievers we've discussed, ones that have been opportunities in disguise. Norm Bobins had a great job at American National Bank and had worked there for fourteen years, but then some changes were made and he was a bit miffed. During this time he received a job offer to be the number two person at a much smaller bank. Norm told me that if he had received the offer six months sooner or six months later, he probably would not have viewed it as an opportunity, since it meant taking a step down, at least in terms of the size of bank. At the time, though, he was alert for alternatives to the position he was in, so when the offer was made he accepted it. As it happened, this was the turning point of his career, a chance to move from a number two to number one job and to use his own strategy to help a bank grow by leaps and bounds.

Art Frigo was in his early thirties and had moved from a consulting firm to work as a special assistant to the president for one of the firm's clients. He was happy in this corporate job, and at one point the president put him in charge of eight of the companies that weren't performing well and asked him to help turn them around. It was a tremendous challenge, but through astute analysis, consolidation, and cost-cutting, Art met the challenge.

Then the company president became sick and a new person stepped into the job. Art hated his new boss, who he termed "rude and crude," and he told me, "I decided that I wasn't as in control of my situation as I thought. I didn't want to turn fifty and feel like I needed this job." At this low point in his career, Art was forced to think outside the box. He came up with the "radical" notion that he might buy the business. At the time, the concept of a leveraged buyout was virtually unheard of. Nonetheless, Art came up with an innovative financing strategy that became one of the first leveraged buyouts in the country, using Citibank's new asset-based practice to help him. This unusual strategy launched Art's entrepreneurial career. With hindsight, he says, "Bad moments can catalyze your career. They wake you up and give you the energy to pursue opportunities you might have missed."

I experienced a similar "bad moment" in one of my first ad agency jobs at Edward H. Weiss & Company. I was working on the Mogen David account, and we were assigned to create a commercial for Mogen David Dry Wines. The underlying marketing premise of the spot was that the target audience—less sophisticated wine drinkers—didn't know which wine to bring as a gift when they visited another person's home. To pay off this premise, the commercial featured a French chef talking about wine; the gimmick was that the chef spoke entirely in French, with his words translated in subtitles.

From the beginning, I protested against this concept. I thought it was ludicrous and that our target audience would not be able to relate to it. The other people on the account dismissed my concerns. The commercial was made, and I stood in the back of the conference room when it was shown in the agency for the first time, before the client had a chance to review it. After the spot finished and the lights came on, I spoke up and said that I had trouble reading the subtitles on the large screen in the conference room and that I assumed viewers would have even more trouble reading them on their smaller television screens. Lee King, the president of the agency, was in the conference room, and he abruptly ended the meeting, turned to me, and said, "I want to see you in my office right now." I followed him back to his office and he slammed the door, saying, "Don't you ever comment on creative! That's not your job!" I told him, "Lee, it's wrong." He told me it was not for me to say.

I walked out of his office and said to myself, "I have to get out of here."

The expected opportunity would have been a bigger and better ad agency along the lines of J. Walter Thompson. It would also have been the wrong opportunity. At that point in my career, I possessed the confidence of youth without the wisdom of experience. No doubt, I would have made enemies at a large agency and the political infighting would have spelled my doom. As Art Frigo says, "Bad experiences wake you up and give you energy to find new opportunities."

The new opportunity I discovered was completely unexpected and not one a career coach might have recommended. I had a friend, Jimmy Rose, who worked for Rhodes Pharmacal, a small family business. Their main product was Donatelli Honey and Egg Facial. When Jimmy offered me the position of marketing director, I knew that some might consider it a lateral move or even a step backward. At the same time, I was twenty-five and needed to learn a lot. I figured working on the client side would help me be a better agency person. I also was looking forward to doing everything from purchasing to planning, a requirement of this job. And I saw that I would be allowed to make mistakes without being cut off at the knees, since I possessed marketing knowledge that no one else at Rhodes had. I told myself, "In the land of the blind, the one-eyed man is king," and took the job. What I didn't know was that this unexpected opportunity would lead to another unexpected opportunity—A. Eicoff & Co. was the ad agency for Rhodes.

Opportunities aren't limited to jobs with other companies. They can also exist within an organization. Unfortunately, when people consider internal opportunities, they usually only look up. Sometimes they need to look sideways or see the hidden opportunities that most people miss. For instance, people can capitalize on seemingly mundane tasks and use them to demonstrate their value to the company. Sam Morasca, the Shell vice president, talked about the importance of doing more than people expect as a way to show management that you have something to contribute. Early in his career at Shell, he was asked to prepare a report analyzing data for use in a senior executive meeting. His boss explained what to do and Sam saw what his predecessor had done, but he also noticed that some interesting data was being ignored. It meant more work, but Sam decided to incorporate the new data into the report, and his efforts were immediately appreciated and commented on in the senior executive meeting.

"I didn't necessarily want to stand out," Sam said. "But I was always looking for ways to blow up the standard model and do things differently and better."

Look for assignments and situations in which you can demonstrate the following three qualities, even if the assignments and situations don't appear all that attractive initially.

1. LEADERSHIP.

It may be nothing more than an opportunity to plan a group or team outing or the chance to be in charge of a relatively unimportant project, but this is the time to step up and show that you can manage other people. It may seem like a little thing, but if your willingness to take charge of small projects and secondary teams becomes a pattern, people will notice.

2. CREATIVITY.

Really smart people are not always very creative. They may be brilliant at figuring out complex strategies or memorizing a ton of data, but they don't always see new or cutting-edge approaches. Over time, you're going to become familiar with the processes and procedures of any job. You should be asking yourself, "Is there a way to improve this process or procedure?" It doesn't have to be a huge issue, and you don't have to reinvent the wheel. It may be something as simple as coming up with a two-step approval process that works faster than the traditional three-step approval process. It may involve figuring out a way to improve your group's video conferencing capabilities by researching new video conferencing providers and adopting a technique or adapting a tool that will enhance the effectiveness of your conferencing efforts.

3. EXECUTION.

There are tasks in every department, team, and group that are difficult or that no one wants to do. They may be time consuming or involve overcoming obstacles, but they must get done. It may be something as clerical as making complex travel arrangements so your whole team can arrive at a given location at the right time. It may be writing a convincing proposal designed to obtain funding approval for your department's new computer system. If you can demonstrate an ability to accomplish these tasks, your ability to execute will be noticed.

Software entrepreneur Flip Filipowski is positively eloquent on this subject. At the start of his career he quickly became a master at executing small but noticeable tasks, and as a result he became chief information officer of A.B. Dick at age twenty-two. Here is how Flip describes his "just do it" mentality: "For two years, I did all the jobs in the IT department that no one else wanted to do. I attacked them with a vengeance, knocking out twenty jobs in one day, and some of them were weeklong or monthlong projects. I just made it my challenge to do them faster. I had no college education and I was competing with guys from Ivy League schools, but I got the CIO job and they didn't.

"Understand that these aren't the popular jobs, and they may lead to dead ends. They carry the risk of failure, and they're difficult. But people take them on as a challenge, and even when they fail at some of them, that's fine, because you're not supposed to do marvelous things with them. And if you succeed even marginally, it looks like you hit a grand slam. It's easier to compete on this level with someone who is an intellectual powerhouse—he won't even take on these types of jobs. In any organization with a hierarchy, this is the best way to get noticed."

Unexpected opportunities also emerge through networking. I am not a joiner by nature, but I recognized early on at Eicoff that as a specialized agency we were somewhat isolated from the larger world of advertising, and made it my business to join outside organizations. Over the years, I've been an active participant in the Young Presidents' Organization and the Direct Marketing Association. I have served on university and corporate boards and have spoken to many advertising and marketing associations. I recognize that when you're starting out some of these opportunities aren't available to you, but many others are. You have the chance to join volunteer or charitable groups associated with your company or industry; you can participate in local and national trade groups; you can become part of networks of professionals similar to yourself (based on age, gender, area of specialization, and so on). Sports-related activities such as golf and tennis outings, perhaps sponsored by industry groups, are also great ways to make valuable connections.

I realize these connections may not seem directly valuable. You may resist them because you tell yourself, "I work hard every day, and I don't feel I should have to work hard after work or on weekends, which I would have to do if I join these groups." If you're a C student, however, these voluntary activities represent some of your best opportunities to forge alliances and make business contacts. You may not possess a ready-made circle of MBAs from a top school to help your career or high-powered connections who will smooth your path. You need to build these connections one person at a time. What you want to avoid at all costs is a "factory mentality." I recall one young executive who was bright and personable and had all the potential in the world, but he insisted on working nine to fve and not one minute more. As a result, he rose to a certain level but never moved beyond it. He never developed a network of outside sources who could help him get business. I'll share with you an expression that you should keep in mind the next time you're considering signing up for one of these activities:

The more people you touch, the more success you'll have.

FIND THE OPPORTUNITIES THAT FIT YOUR PERSONALITY

Now that you're aware of the range and volume of unexpected opportunities that will come your way, the next step is to choose the right ones. You won't have the time and energy to pursue everything, so you need to be selective about which ones you go after. To make the best choices, focus on the types of opportunities that fit your personality and especially your strengths. One top ad agency executive I know—another C student—has especially high emotional intelligence and is good at forming strong, enduring friendships. As a result, he has pursued unexpected opportunities to meet new people and grow his network. Over the years, he has been even more active than I've been in joining industry trade groups, not-for-profit association committees, and men's groups. His network of contacts is probably more extensive and more actively involved in referring potential clients to him than anyone I know.

When my son, Michael, graduated from college and was trying to decide what to do, I sat down with him and we talked about his strengths: his empathy, outgoing personality, and verbal communication skills. Clearly he would make a great salesperson. But Michael also was independent-minded and flourished when he was on his own. When an unexpected opportunity emerged—the chance to be an owner/operator of a hearing-aid distributorship—he grabbed it. Many young people might not see the chance to go into a business with a largely senior citizen customer base as an opportunity. They might not want to work in an environment where they lacked colleagues their own age or the excitement of a large, growing company. Michael, however, flourished in his new job because his strengths were ideally suited to the business. Customers loved his honesty and genuine warmth, and they trusted him enough to make a high-ticket purchase from him. Michael's business has flourished because he found the perfect opportunity for who he is.

Sam Morasca, too, found unexpected opportunities based on his strengths. A former student athlete, Sam is also naturally gregarious and comfortable in group settings. It made sense, then, for Sam to gravitate toward team-based opportunities when he joined Shell. Rather than look for individual chances to display his expertise, he focused on joining teams and helping those teams perform better.

You would expect someone like Sam, who became Shell's head of marketing, to have been promoted as a result of individual accomplishments, but Sam's achievements were team based. It is to Shell's credit that they recognized the value of Sam's particular mix of skills and rewarded him for them.

Flip Filipowski was drawn to opportunities in the software industry that others shunned. Some of the ventures at which Flip has been incredibly successful were barely viewed as opportunities by others because they carried so much risk. Flip's strengths, though, are his vision and his willingness to abide a level of risk that others might find intolerable. As a result, Flip was willing to go where angels fear to tread. He summarizes his philosophy as follows:

"What helped me be so successful are the same things that get me in trouble: fearlessness, the ability to take on any amount of risk, the capacity to face that risk with no panic, and the willingness to persevere regardless of how many failures I have. The person who keeps coming back for more and never gives up no matter what the disaster is the guy who wins. Never ever give up, no matter how beat up you are."

Given this strength, Flip always seems to find unexpected opportunities with high downsize risk and high upside potential.

The following exercise is designed to help you assess your strengths so you can recognize unexpected opportunities that might fit you well:

Start out by listing all your major strengths and weaknesses on a piece of paper. Try to limit each list to five or fewer items and focus on ones that have some bearing on your career (you may be a great tennis player, for instance, but that probably won't influence your career direction). Do not confine this list to traditional academic terms, such as math, science, and so on. Strengths can include everything from an ability to develop and maintain good relationships, to being highly empathetic, to having a knack for problem-solving. After creating your list, do the following:

- Translate your strengths into potential job or career terms. For instance, if one of your strengths is an ability to think on your feet, such a strength might help you as a salesperson. List at least three potential jobs/careers for each strength.

- Translate your weaknesses into potential job or career terms. For instance, if you're not a good communicator or relationship builder, you won't make a very good salesperson. List all the jobs and careers that seem ill-suited to you, given your weaknesses.

- Based on your translated strengths and weaknesses, create a list of internal and external opportunities that might come your way and that you should be alert for. Remember, these should not be limited to traditional job offers but include everything from assignments related to your current job, to industry association memberships, to workshops and seminars.

- Based on your weaknesses, create a list of activities and assignments that make no sense for you to pursue.

PASS ON THE MONEY, TAKE THE EXPERIENCE

When considering unexpected opportunities, eliminate a money-first attitude, at least during the first ten years of your career. I know that money is important, and you're going to have A student friends who are being offered jobs upon graduation from MBA programs and law schools that pay unbelievable amounts of money. Resist the temptation to take high-paying jobs just because they're high paying. If you don't, you'll regret the decision down the line. If you gain the right experience early on, you'll have more than ample opportunities to make up the pay gap with A students.

It took me a good ten years before I made decent money in my career. At Heinz, Edward H. Weiss, and Rhodes Pharmacal I received low to middling salaries. Even during my early years at Eicoff I received a relatively low salary. If, however, I had missed any of these experiences, I would never have earned what I earned later on in my career. Like many young people, I didn't know the exact knowledge and skills that would help me further my career, but I did know that all three jobs offered great learning opportunities. If I had had a crystal ball and could see that I would be a CEO, I could have targeted jobs that allowed me to gain conflict resolution, negotiating, and a variety of leadership skills. In lieu of this crystal ball, I had a sense that being on the client side was a good idea, and that Rhodes Pharmacal would give me a chance to do everything—purchasing, human resources, selling, operations, financial. I could have been paid two or three times as much to be a specialist at a large ad agency, but I would have learned half as much. The lesson is not to judge opportunities by their monetary value but by the potential value of the experiences to your career.

Art Frigo is a great believer of putting experience before money early in one's career. As he says, "Early on, people make the mistake of asking, 'How much does this job pay?' They should be asking, 'Is this job going to provide me with experiences that will lead me to the career I want?'

"After two years of working for experience, people start noticing you. At that point, you may receive an offer from a competitor for 15 percent more money. You say to yourself, 'I could use the extra ten thousand.' But an extra ten thousand dollars isn't going to change your life."

Art has a great rule of thumb for changing jobs. He believes that you should change jobs only when your growth—your learning and development—starts leveling off. At that point, he feels you should reposition yourself within the company in order to gain more responsibility for fresh challenges, or you must leave.

Focusing on the experience rather than the money is tough for many C students, but if you're smart about gaining the right experience, you will find that you're ready to handle bigger jobs for more money later on. In fact, if you've been astute about gaining the right experiences, you'll be in a better position for many big jobs than those A students who have done well as specialists but lack the broader experiences most big jobs demand. Many management and leadership positions require a diverse range of expertise and experience, and if you're always taking narrowly focused jobs, you'll miss out on a lot of low-end skills (i.e., people skills) that you'll need later in your career. You may be a great financial analyst, but you'll be hopeless when it comes to negotiating a deal.

Be aware that unexpected opportunities often involve less pay than the expected ones. If you're following a linear progression in your career, you do one job well and another company offers you more money to do the same job well. C students, though, may bounce from one unexpected opportunity to the next, and one job may involve responsibilities that aren't even relevant to the next job. Recognize that you're going to be climbing many learning curves, and while you may not always be well compensated for the climb at the beginning, you will be later on.

DON'T BE AFRAID OF THE UNEXPECTED OPPORTUNITY

Perhaps more than the lack of money, a great opportunity may turn you off because it seems scary. By "scary" I mean that it requires you to take a position or even enter a field where you lack the necessary knowledge. In reality, you probably possess at least some of the knowledge you need to do a job, but you're missing something that makes the position seem intimidating. When I was hired by Al Eicoff, my main responsibility was generating new business, something I had never done before. Those first six months were terrifying, especially when Al would ask daily, "Get any new business yet?" At first I didn't know where to begin. I might as well have been cold calling Procter & Gamble to ask for their account. What I came to understand, though, is that most business skills aren't rocket science and that any motivated C student can overcome his lack of knowledge and become competent.

Still, I didn't know this at the time I accepted the Eicoff position. What helped me overcome my fear was that the opportunity felt right. Logically, I knew that many smaller companies didn't have big ad budgets but had good products; that they were looking for an inexpensive, results-producing method of marketing those products; and Eicoff's television advertising approach met their needs. I also was aware that Al needed help. As brilliant as he was, he required someone who could complement him, and my relationship-building skills and other competencies dovetailed perfectly with his. It was unlikely that I would ever find someone who not only wanted but needed a "junior partner" as much as Al wanted and needed me. Finally, I trusted my instinct. As I emphasized in an earlier chapter, you have to trust what your gut tells you, and my gut told me that once I was able to crack the code of new business, the job would be nirvana.

So don't be intimidated by unexpected opportunities just because you're going to be asked to do something you've never done before. In the business world there is a formal name for these types of opportunities—stretch assignments. Organizations purposefully assign people tasks they know they're not qualified to handle, but they do so in the hope that people will stretch themselves and grow into the job.

If the opportunity is right for you, trust that you can make the stretch and take full advantage of the opportunity. CEO Louise O'Sullivan made the transition from being a teacher to working for Groen, a foodservice company and a division of the Dover Corporation, now a $6 billion company. At first she was writing technical manuals, so not only was she in a completely different environment, but she was writing about totally unfamiliar technical issues. As scary as this must have been for Louise, she, too, was strongly motivated by the opportunity and her sense that this was the right situation for her. She quickly diminished her fear of the unknown by not only mastering the technical knowledge she needed but the application knowledge as well. She made it her business to talk to people in the field and the shop floor so that she would understand how her company's products—steam kettles, braising pans, and other foodservice institutional equipment—worked. What made their braising pans better than the competitor's? While the engineers knew what their steam kettles were made of and why they were more durable than other steam kettles, Louise found out how fast they cooked and how versatile they were.

More unexpected opportunities followed. The vice president of sales wanted Louise to travel with the manufacturer reps, assuming that her growing knowledge of how the company's products worked might help her connect with the customer. Having absolutely no customer experience must have made this assignment seem extremely difficult to her. It probably also didn't help that her direct boss, the national sales manager, didn't approve of this plan, telling Lou e that since the reps were all men and so were the customers, she might not fit in. Though Louise pointed out that some of the school foodservice directors and other food and beverage managers were women, her boss still resisted sending Louise out with the reps. Finally, he conceded but insisted that she concentrate on Louisiana, where "if she messed up, she wouldn't do much harm."

In fact, she was highly successful with the reps. She was eventually promoted to national sales manager and then vice president of sales. In that latter position, she discovered that some of the company's products were outdated, and she began complaining about their flaws and suggesting new models and product improvements. Her boss, impressed by her criticisms and innovative suggestions, told her he was making her vice president of sales and engineering. She would be replacing the former V.P. of engineering, who had been there thirty years. On top of that, Louise would be in charge of highly talented, veteran engineers but lacked an engineering background. The engineers no doubt resented both her lack of expertise and her replacing their boss of thirty years. Louise recalled that their attitude was, "Don't tell us what to design, Ms. Marketing person."

While this unexpected opportunity might have been intimidating to some, Louise attacked it with gusto. Instead of design knowledge, she brought a sense of excitement, field experience, and urgency to her job, and this eventually won over the people in her department. She brought in outside consultants to help with the design work, and that fresh thinking resulted in new, successful products. Rather than be intimidated by what she didn't know and refusing to take on the engineering position, Louise recognized it as a great opportunity to prove herself. Because she was able to do so, she was soon named president of the company.

Perhaps CDW founder Mike Krasny best exemplifies what can happen if you're not afraid when opportunities present themselves. In 1984 Mike clearly saw a gap in the tech market. He realized that given the rising demand for personal computers and the relative lack of low-end products, a huge market might exist for reselling computers. The only problem was that he had no experience as a marketer or in operations. He knew a great deal about technology primarily through self-education, but his previous job experience largely involved selling Toyotas for his father, who ran a car dealership. Nonetheless, his passion for the business and conviction that he had glimpsed a major trend motivated him to found the business in his parents' kitchen, selling his first computer for $200 through a *Chicago Tribune* classified ad. From there he progressed to selling used computers out of his car trunk. In a relatively short period of time CDW became a $1 billion plus company with thousands of employees and Michael was named Entrepreneur of the Year by *Inc.* magazine. He embraced the opportunity and learned on the job, unwilling to be stopped by all the things he didn't know.

Art Frigo takes this whole concept of unexpected opportunities one step further. When he was at 3M he positioned himself for jobs that he wasn't qualified for in the technical sense of the term. Though he wasn't a sales supervisor, he was involved in informal projects where he was in charge of other salespeople, and he used this informal experience to bolster his credentials. His belief is that people are more qualified for "next level up" jobs than they give themselves credit for. Though they may not have had formal job responsibilities and clear-cut experience to qualify them for a higher-level position, they probably have been involved in tasks and assignments that have given them knowledge and skills that will be useful at that new level. For this reason Art advocates using both informal and formal experience as leverage to capitalize on unexpected opportunities.

A TEN-YEAR WINDOW FOR OPPORTUNITIES

Give yourself ten years to watch for and capitalize on all types of unexpected opportunities. During this time your goal should be to make yourself as marketable as possible, to match or exceed what your A student colleagues know. If you have doubts, remind yourself that the more experiences you have in a variety of areas, the greater chance you have of succeeding. Contrary to what many people believe, you don't have to follow a narrow career path to reach the top. Your career may hinge on volunteering for a task no one else wants to do or taking a job at a smaller company for less money. Your unexpected opportunity may involve playing golf with someone, forming a friendship with that person, and receiving a terrific job offer from his company five years later. You never know where your unexpected opportunities will emerge, so it's key to keep an open mind and not rule potential opportunities out because they don't fit a narrow definition of opportunity. You never know which contact you make, knowledge you acquire, or skill you master will be critical for job success. When you look around and see people your age making a lot more money than you, repeat the following to yourself:

It's not where you begin, but where you end up.

Finally, to take full advantage of unexpected opportunities, ask yourself the following questions:

- Am I thinking about opportunities in the broadest possible way? Am I making sure I don't rule out chances to learn and grow just because they aren't traditional opportunities?

- When I receive a job offer, am I considering more than the money or prestige of the company or job title before making my decision? Am I looking at how the job will help me become more marketable? If I were offered a job with a smaller company for less money but with a chance to learn a new, key skill, would I take it?

- Am I alert for opportunities? Am I regularly looking for chances to develop my skills, contacts, and knowledge through work assignments, charitable projects, academic classes, training programs, jobs with other companies, and other ways?

- Would I be willing to take on an assignment or job even if I felt I lacked the knowledge and skills I needed to do it well right from the start?

- Do I consider whether an opportunity makes sense for me based on my strengths or whether I should avoid it because of my weaknesses? Do I evaluate it based on whether it will help me achieve long-range career goals or just from a short-term standpoint? Do I rely on my instinct to tell me if I should reject one opportunity and pursue another?

Use these questions as a continuous litmus test for opportunities, and you will likely make good decisions when these types of opportunities unexpectedly arise.

CHAPTER 7

SELL WHAT YOU BELIEVE

Selling levels the playing field. By that I mean that if you can sell, it doesn't matter where you went to school or how many false career starts you've made. Everyone has the potential to be a great salesperson, but not everyone develops this ability. C students must recognize that if they can learn to sell with conviction, they can dramatically improve their career prospects.

It shouldn't come as any surprise that some of the best salespeople are C students. Instinctively, they recognize that selling is their ticket to the top. As a result, they work hard developing their ability to communicate with sincerity and purpose, convincing others that they can trust them. Their credibility in the eyes of prospects and customers is far higher than that of someone who sells intelligently but coldly.

This chapter, though, is about more than being a good salesperson in the traditional sense of the term. Many of you work in jobs that have nothing to do with sales per se. On the other hand, you're selling all the time. You need to sell your boss on the chance to work on a key project. You have to sell your direct reports on putting in more time and energy than usual to meet a tough deadline. You must sell a supplier on being a true partner with your company. You need to sell colleagues on a risky but potentially highly profitable strategy.

Selling is a multifaceted skill that can help you in every aspect of your job and your career. Even if you don't view yourself as a particularly good salesperson, you can develop this skill to the point that you can sell effectively on a number of levels. Remember, however, that you will be effective only if you sell honestly, passionately, and with a sense of purpose.

CHOOSING THE RIGHT MOMENT AND THE RIGHT CAUSE

If you're not in a sales position and you're just getting started in your career, you may wonder when you're going to have the chance to sell anyone anything. Let me assure you that you're going to be selling regularly. You'll find that you need to convince someone of something almost every week. It could be a minor matter of lobbying for a new software system or making a major presentation to senior staff. Whatever it is, you must articulate your point of view in a convincing manner so that someone in power buys it.

Some people make the mistake of overestimating the value of their ideas. They are the ones who in school were always raising their hands and at work are always forcing their opinions on others. Some of their ideas may be excellent, but these good ideas get lost amid all the bad or mediocre ones. They are in love with the sound of their voice, and this irritating quality makes them less effective at selling even their best concepts. People tune them out before they have a chance to explain their ideas fully.

When you're just starting out and have no credibility based on past accomplishments, you need to be selective about when you venture an opinion or propose an idea. Wait until you have an epiphany or something close to it—you realize you've just discovered a way to get something done faster, better, or cheaper. You have great faith in your idea and its viability, and you are itching to tell someone about it. Maybe you go in and propose the idea to your boss or speak up during a meeting, but you allow your belief in the idea to drive your words.

Earlier I mentioned that at my first ad agency job I worked on the Mogen David account. The president of the company was Ben Wernick, an intimidating man who accentuated this trait by sitting on a raised chair at meetings so he could look down on his audience. During meetings no one was allowed to speak without first raising a hand and being called on. I was afraid to open my mouth, and so for the first five or six months I didn't say one word in meetings.

Mr. Wernick had been obsessed with the success of a competitive product, Richard's Wild Irish Rose, which had captured a significant percentage of the low-end market. Its success was due in large part to its 20 percent alcohol by volume, while Mogen David's beverage was only 12 percent alcohol by volume. Our research showed that people preferred the taste of Mogen David to Richard's Wild Irish Rose, but they bought the latter because of the higher alcohol percentage. Consequently, Mogen David decided to introduce a product that was also 20 percent alcohol by volume. I had a brainstorm during a meeting to determine the name for this new product. I thought of the perfect name, and I was so convinced that it was the right one that I raised my hand.

Ben Wernick had been speaking, and when he saw my hand go up he stopped talking in mid-sentence, pointed at me and said, "You! You, the one who never speaks."

"Mr. Wernick," I said, "I think we should call it MD 20/20. Because it's 20 percent alcohol by volume."

For a moment no one said anything. Then Mr. Wernick turned and said, "I can hear it now; people are going to go into liquor stores and say, 'Give me some of that 20/20.'"

MD 20/20 was born, and from that moment on Mr. Wernick loved me. I have no doubt that I sold him in part because I was selective about when I spoke, and in part because I was absolutely convinced it was the best name for the product.

To sell selectively and effectively, here are some dos and don'ts for you to follow:

DO:

- Wait until you're firmly convinced you have an idea or solution that is absolutely right for a given situation.

- Think about what is the best time and place for voicing your idea.

- Rehearse what it is you want to propose so that you articulate it succinctly when you choose to speak.

- Give yourself permission to speak from your heart rather than just from your head; allow people to see that you really care about the issue.

DON'T:

- Feel you have to come up with a new idea or give your opinion at every meeting you attend.

- Believe that being professional means arguing for your position without betraying any emotion.

- Fake being excited about an idea or approach that you really have no enthusiasm for.

FIND YOUR BEST WAY OF SELLING

Everyone has his or her own way of selling, and I'm not suggesting you need to adopt my approach (in fact, my approach to selling has changed over the years—no one would accuse me of being reluctant to voice my ideas these days). Some people make their points with great drama, while others are more effective with a low-key demeanor. Either is fine, as long as you believe in what you're selling. Contrary to what you might think, your audience can sense when you're not sincere. Perhaps you don't look people in the eye when you speak. Maybe you mumble. It's possible that you're a good actor and sound like you mean what you're saying, but your body language betrays you. It is very difficult to fool people consistently, and is especially difficult to fool a boss or customer who knows you well. Therefore, don't feign enthusiasm for a program that leaves you cold or volunteer ideas that you believe are suspect. If you are dealing with a client or customer, don't try to sell her a service about which you harbor doubts. Most of all, sell in a way that feels comfortable to you rather than in a manner that is comfortable for someone else.

Early in their careers many people have a fixed idea in their minds of how they should act in an organizational setting, and this often involves conforming to certain stereotypes. They believe that to sell effectively they must be highly aggressive and never take no for an answer. They think that they must never show weakness or admit that they were wrong. Obviously, some successful salespeople do fit this profile. If, however, these traits make you uncomfortable and don't fit your personality, you shouldn't feel they are the only way you can sell yourself or your company's products and services.

For instance, I have found that admitting to a mistake helps strengthen relationships and increases sales credibility. Clearly you don't want to be admitting to and apologizing for mistakes all the time, since that would indicate you are careless and incompetent. On the other hand, being brave enough to admit an error every once in a while communicates that you're honest. It communicates that you trust the other person enough to admit that what you did was wrong.

One of our clients is Bose Electronics, a company founded by Dr. Amar Bose. A number of years back, Dr. Bose wanted our agency to create television commercials for their Wave radio. Dr. Bose came to Chicago and made a presentation to our creative group. Some of our creatives felt that it wouldn't work, and I told Dr. Bose it would be a tough sell, but we would try to do our best. He thanked me for being honest and said they would create the commercial in-house and requested that we handle only the media buying part of the campaign. We did so, and to my surprise it was a huge success. Once we knew it had been successful, I called Dr. Bose and apologized, saying, "We were wrong." To this day, Dr. Bose tells this story and says that I'm the only ad executive he ever met who admitted that he had made a mistake.

It may take a little time, but you need to figure out the best way to present ideas and ask for things from people you work with. To give you a sense of the range of options available to you, let me give you a profile of the selling styles of a couple of our high achievers, along with several other types of styles.

Sam Morasca sold himself and his ideas primarily within one organization—Shell. During his twenty-five years there, he had sixteen different jobs. In most cases, he had to make a good argument for why he was the best candidate for the position he aspired to. Sometimes his argument was directly to the person inter-

viewing candidates, and in other instances it was a result of his efforts to build what he termed his profile within Shell. He was astute at knowing what type of profile made you a good candidate
for executive positions, and he made it his business to acquire the
expertise and experience that fit the profile.

For instance, he saw that engineers occupied all the senior-
level positions at Shell. Lacking this credential, he recognized that
he needed technical experience within the company. It was similar to when he was in the air force, where he saw that only flyers
become top generals. Sam knew that all the senior people had at
some point in their Shell careers run a refinery or chemical plant,
and Sam, with the help of his mentor, became the first nonengineer to become a plant operations manager. When he took over
the job, his plant superintendent was terrified that Sam would
screw up in some way because of his lack of technical training,
but Sam reassured him, saying, "Don't worry. I won't start turning
any valves or flipping any switches." Because Sam was already skilled
at managing people and processes, he was able to handle the job,
and the credential was so important that years later people simply
assumed he was an engineer because of this plant manager position.

By keeping his eyes focused on his profile, Sam moved from
one great job to the next. He was chosen to do distribution planning in a joint venture with the Saudis, then was picked to be
head of domestic trading and crude oil supply, a hot job at Shell.
Later he moved to London and became head of international trading, which positioned him perfectly for Shell's top marketing job.

Sam built his profile and sold himself by being down to earth,
friendly, and a great team player. His supreme likability and competency made people with job openings want to hire him. He
moved upward not by being a show-off, individual star but by quietly planning his moves and selling himself through deeds rather
than words.

Larry Levy sells with passion and honesty. He has built a real estate and food empire by focusing on areas he knows and loves and by preserving a reputation for being a highly ethical businessperson. If one of Larry's chefs comes up with a wonderful new soup recipe, he will call you on the phone and say, "You've got to come over and try our soup." And he will be hovering nearby and asking even before you've had your second spoonful, "Isn't it great?"

At the same time, he never overhypes his ventures and is scrupulous about disclosing every relevant piece of information—both pro and con—to investors before he accepts their money. He is the type of entrepreneur that everyone wants to do business with; he doesn't have to sell them so much as present them with an opportunity.

People wonder how Larry managed to convince so many ballparks and other entertainment venues to hire his gourmet food-service company. The assumption is that he must have had to do a lot of hard selling to achieve this coup. The actual story provides some insight into his selling style.

"When we started out, we were building one restaurant at a time, two or three new ones each year. It was the hardest, dumbest way to make a living. One bad restaurant kills two good ones, and it's devastating to your emotions. At the time, the White Sox built the first sky boxes at Comiskey Park in Chicago. They built twenty-seven, got limited partners in the team to lease five of them, but couldn't get anyone else to take the other ones. The White Sox thought if they could get a restaurant to cater the sky boxes, they might have a better chance of filling them, and that's when they approached us. At first, we said we don't do that, we're fine-dining people, we're not institutional caterers. We turned them down three times.

"Finally, they agreed to let us do the catering as a real restaurateur would, and they told us they would provide us with great seats for the game. Being big baseball fans, we said we'd do it. We said yes for all the wrong reasons, and now it's 90 percent of our business."

Larry clearly relishes telling this story. Rather than talking about his foresight and business acumen, he makes it seem as if he stumbled onto this formula for success. This humility and honesty make Larry someone people trust implicitly, and it is why he is able to get deals done that others can't.

Sam and Larry represent just two selling styles out of an infinite variety. Both of them found a style that fit their personalities relatively early in their careers, and stuck with it. Your goal, then, is to find the selling style that suits you. To help you do so, I've distilled some of the most common styles into the following descriptions. See if you can find the one that is closest to your personality.

Quiet Style

You are more comfortable making a point or conducting a sale one-on-one rather than in a group. You may pass on asking for something or making a bold statement if you're not 100 percent convinced it is of critical importance. You tend to be low-key rather than a ball of energy when you're selling, and you expect your audience to be swayed by what you say rather than by the force of your personality. In some instances, you prefer making a written argument rather than a verbal one. At the same time, when you say something, people pay attention to you. You can be quietly forceful when you believe something should be done, conveying the force of your belief with the tone of your voice and your body language.

Humorous Style

Though you can be serious, humor is essential to how you sell. You can poke fun of yourself and joke with your prospects, customers, and boss. In this way you diminish the tension in certain selling situations and create an atmosphere in which it's easier to get a deal done. By not taking yourself too seriously, you earn a reputation as someone who is fun to work with, an attribute that can help you be chosen for teams and projects where the manager wants people who are enjoyable to be around. Having a humorous style does not mean being frivolous and superficial. Like anything else, too much humor can work against you. As a result, you know when humor is appropriate and when a more serious approach is called for.

Charming Style

Charm can manifest itself in a number of different ways. You might be a great storyteller who can entertain an individual or larger audience with wonderful anecdotes; you use these stories to make your points as well as to entertain. You might be debonair or worldly, able to talk about anything with anyone. You dress beautifully and have style; people buy your ideas and accede to your requests because you are so attractively self-assured. At its best, charm translates into charisma, and people usually want to do business with anyone who is charismatic. Remember, though, that charm will take you only so far and no further. At a certain point you'll hit the wall if you don't have substance to back up this style.

Networking Style

You make connections and establish relationships in order to accomplish your goals. Your strength is building a network both within your organization and outside of it and leveraging this network expertly. This means you both ask for favors and do favors for others, turning these relationships into win-win situations. You regularly receive referrals for outside sales. Internally, you are able to obtain resources when others come up empty, drawing on your network of people to achieve objectives.

Direct Style

You don't mince words or hesitate to ask for something you need. You are perfectly willing to communicate your request to a CEO, customer, or anyone else, and your directness is often refreshing to people used to vague or manipulative requests. Your honesty and openness stand you in good stead when dealing with prospective clients who appreciate straight talk. While you may not be a storyteller or a charmer, you compensate by getting to points quickly and explaining situations clearly and compellingly. The caveat here is that being overly direct can turn people off. This style works best when it is accompanied by sensitivity to an audience's concerns.

It's likely that none of these styles fits you perfectly. Most of us use at least two or three of these styles in different situations, adapting or blending them for maximum effectiveness. In fact, having a flexible style is great. You need to know, for instance, when humor is inappropriate and when a direct style will work best with a particular customer. At the same time, don't try to be all things to all people. Just because you're a C student doesn't mean you have to try to please everyone, being the person you think others want you to be. Use your natural personality and build on it to create a distinctive selling style that feels comfortable to you.

SELLING AS A PROCESS: LEARNING THROUGH TRIAL AND ERROR

Some young people, especially C students, bring a classroom mentality to their jobs. They think in terms of quarters or semesters rather than years and fear they're failures when they don't make an immediate sale. It's highly unlikely they're going to receive an A in selling after being with a company for a few months, or even a few years. At the same time, they can make steady improvements that eventually will help them become superior at selling themselves and selling to others. The following seven suggestions are ones you can put into practice over time:

1. PAY ATTENTION TO HOW OTHER PEOPLE SELL.

As you know, I place great faith in the C student's powers of observation. No matter where you work, you have at least one or two colleagues (or bosses) who are skillful salespeople. Pay close attention to how they handle themselves in the following situations:

- Making presentations to a team or other internal groups.

- Meeting with prospective clients or customers.

- Attempting to sell additional products or services to existing clients or customers.

- Convincing a boss to take a specific action.

- Helping colleagues reach consensus on an issue under discussion.

What do they do that you respect and admire? What specific approaches do they use that help them achieve their goals? Do you notice certain traits and techniques that you might incorporate into your repertoire? On the negative side, what do they do that you dislike or find off-putting? Do they handle themselves in a way that you find phony or ill suited to who you are?

In answering these questions you can use your observations to evolve your selling approach. Again, this is not going to happen overnight. If, however, you make it a habit to observe how a variety of people sell, you will find that you can adopt and adapt best practices.

2. PAY ATTENTION TO HOW OTHER PEOPLE TRY TO SELL TO YOU.

Even when you're not a top-level executive, people are trying to sell you something all the time. In the course of a given workday you probably receive at least one call from someone offering a business service, usually a vendor or supplier. Depending on your job, you may also be on the receiving end of presentations from vendors or suppliers. Outside work, you find yourself in a buying position when you're looking at cars, searching for a financial adviser, or shopping for clothes. Who do you think does the best job of selling? Who does the worst job? Think about the good and bad qualities they exhibit and remind yourself of what those qualities are when you're attempting to make a sale. Most of all, decide whether they appear to be telling you the truth or handing you a line. In selling situations people often pay a great deal of attention to what they say but relatively little attention to their credibility. Credibility, though, is absolutely paramount. Watch salespeople attempting to get you to buy something and determine whether they are sincere.

3. DON'T MAKE THE SAME MISTAKE TWICE.

Or to put it another way, don't be a know-it-all who refuses to acknowledge his mistakes or blames his shortcomings on others.

As a humble C student, recognize that to err is human, and you're going to err in selling situations. You may come off as too aggressive and turn off a prospect. You may be too forceful in asking your boss for a promotion and cause her to turn you down. You may adopt a style that you think is appropriate for selling but is inappropriate for you. Whatever your mistake is, acknowledge it and make it a priority not to repeat it. During the first five or ten years of my career I must have made a thousand mistakes, but I made very few of them a second time.

4. PLANT SEEDS.

Just as learning to sell can be a process, making a sale can also involve a series of steps. You may be convinced that you're ready to be promoted or that a customer should buy an additional service, but if you simply ask for the order, you'll be turned down. Many people aren't ready to buy what you're selling and need to be conditioned before they see the validity of your position. Therefore, plant seeds.

For instance, when current vice president Kelly Dulin first joined A. Eicoff & Co., she set a record for the time it took to move from media assistant to media buyer. She planted a number of seeds in the minds of her bosses that suggested she had the talent necessary for jobs with greater responsibility. I recall the day when she planted such a seed with me. I was walking by the media assistant bullpen and Kelly called out to me, "I understand you went to the University of Arizona. Do you want to make a little bet?" The Arizona football team was playing the University of Illinois team that weekend. I asked her what she wanted to bet, and Kelly told me, "A cup of coffee." I told her she was on.

I don't remember who won the bet, but I do remember thinking that she was different in a positive way. For one thing, she had taken the time to learn where I had gone to college. For another, she was not intimidated by the CEO and broke the ice appropriately. Third, she knew that win or lose, she would give herself the opportunity to have coffee with the CEO, a smart way of building the relationship.

Planting seeds can be as simple as telling your boss, "I know I'm not ready to be a vice president yet, but I want you to know that's what I aspire to." It can involve saying to a customer, "You may not be able to make the investment in product X today, but I just want to tell you about it for future reference." Once you plant these seeds, they germinate on their own. It's much better for your customers and bosses to discover for themselves that you're the right person for the job or that they must purchase product X.

5. MAKE PEOPLE FEEL SAFE.

Never underestimate the anxiety people have about their jobs. When you're trying to convince them to do something—to give you a transfer, to add an additional service—they often are thinking to themselves, "If this doesn't work out, how will it affect me?" Most companies are volatile places these days, and no one wants to be the one who made a decision that hurt their companies. When I meet with prospective clients, I always attempt to convey the message that "You can't afford *not* to hire us." When they choose an ad agency, they want the one that gives them the best chance for success. If the agency fails, they could lose their jobs. Therefore, the sales presentation must make it safe for them. They need to believe that the agency will do more than any of its competitors to succeed. Convince them that your agency gives them the best chance to succeed and you greatly increase the odds of winning the account.

Try to help people feel safe with whatever decision you hope they'll make. If they're considering hiring you for a key job, let them know that you will do whatever it takes—coming in on weekends, making cold calls, checking your work three times to make sure there are no errors—to make their decision to hire you look good. To do this, you need to be perceptive about what they fear most if they do what you suggest. In their minds, what is the worst-case scenario? You need to address this fear and make them feel reasonably certain it won't come to pass.

6. BE A PROFESSIONAL.

This simple piece of advice is often overlooked by sellers. I cannot tell you how many job candidates and vendors have come into our offices and been unprofessional in some way. They've worn inappropriate clothing, avoided eye contact, displayed lousy posture, and spoken ungrammatically. This last point may seem trivial, but it connotes a sloppiness in thought that might translate into work situations. Even if you were an average student at an average school, you can still speak proper English. When someone says to me, "I seen that," or upon meeting me for the first time exclaims, "What's happening?" I dismiss them immediately. My mother came to the United States when she was eleven, and English was her second language, but when I was growing up, she would always correct me if I made a grammatical mistake. "Who!" she would tell me, "not whom!" If she could master the language, you can master it sufficiently to make your arguments in proper English.

7. LEARN HOW TO PUSH HARD BUT NOT TOO HARD.

You have to develop the instinct of pushing hard but backing off when you sense the other person might say no. Sometimes you are overly aggressive and the strategy backfires, but this failure helps you develop your instinct for when to move forward and when to back off.

Expect to find yourself in situations where you don't know how hard to push it. Don't be surprised if you find you've asked for too much in a salary negotiation or demanded a concession from a supplier and the supplier tells you he doesn't want your business. After a while, you, too, will develop a feel for these situations and become skilled at asking for a lot but knowing when to back off.

SELL THE RIGHT THING

Rich Melman was a Fuller Brush Man when he was young, and by his own admission he was terrible at it. Mike Krasny was not a great car salesman. Art Frigo may have been a decent salesman when he was employed by 3M, but he became a great one when he started his own businesses. Louise O'Sullivan didn't do any selling as a teacher, but when she was given the opportunity to sell for foodservice equipment company Groen, she excelled. Mike Waters turned into a great salesperson as soon as he began selling products he invented.

It doesn't matter whether you're selling products, services, or yourself. If you feel like a fish out of water, you're going to flop. If you believe you're in the perfect environment and that you have a golden opportunity to sell something you really care about, you'll have a great chance to succeed. All the individuals I just mentioned were in the latter category. As soon as they found their niche, they hit their selling stride.

I emphasize this point especially to all you C students out there because an inferiority complex comes with the territory. Al Eicoff, for all his accomplishments, frequently said that he suffered from an inferiority complex. Probably half of the people you've read about in these pages have said words to the effect that they feel like they're fooling everyone, and sooner or later they will be unmasked as imposters. I'm sure a lot of this stems from being a mediocre student, feeling like an outsider (because of gender, upbringing, and so on), or having made some false career starts. On the surface it seems as if everyone else has an advantage.

It is very difficult to sell effectively when you have low self-esteem. You won't ask for a transfer or a raise or dare leave your current employer for a better position if you feel inferior. You can't sell a product or service to anyone if you believe no one will take what you say seriously.

If you're in the wrong situation, your feeling of inadequacy will probably persist. When you don't feel comfortable with a culture or don't have faith in the products and services you're selling, you probably will do a lousy job and your sense of inferiority becomes a self-fulfilling prophecy.

When people like Rich Melman and Mike Krasny found the right situations, they quickly gained confidence. Their passion for what they were selling, combined with running their own business, helped them sell with a conviction that they otherwise might have lacked. Inside, they may have experienced doubts when they started their businesses—I know Rich did, especially when it took a while for R.J. Grunts, his first restaurant, to take off. To this day, Mike is still afraid of failure. These doubts, though, weren't visible to customers, who just noticed his enthusiasm and energy. As insecure as Al Eicoff may have felt, he projected tremendous self-confidence. He used his feelings of inferiority as a catalyst and a challenge to prove himself in every selling situation. It didn't matter if he was selling to the CEO of a Fortune 500 company or a small entrepreneur; he saw each presentation as an opportunity to show he knew more about television advertising and how to make it work than anyone else. Because he loved television advertising in general and his theories about it in particular, he came across to many prospective clients as brilliant. When Al got up on his soapbox and began his spiel, he was mesmerizing.

If you can find your niche the way Al found his, you can be a highly effective salesperson. Perhaps the best story I know of someone finding his niche is Dino Child. Dino is director of player development at the Venetian in Las Vegas, and he is someone who was made for the gaming industry. His grandfather used to run penny and nickel crap games at his dry cleaners in the Bronx before he moved to Las Vegas. Dino and his siblings used to play blackjack to determine who would do the dishes. Growing up in Vegas, Dino loved the excitement and glamour of the casinos. From age fifteen on, he worked in part-time jobs as a busboy and waiter in restaurants attached to the casinos. Nonetheless, he began college intending to major in labor relations and eventually become a lawyer. In college he was making $40,000 in tips alone working part-time, while his friends were graduating from college and happy to get jobs paying $20,000. But Dino found himself drawn to gaming as a career. He didn't fall into the trap of choosing a career that others thought was more respectable than working for a casino. He chose to do what he loved.

As Dino worked his way up from dealer to pit boss to managerial and marketing positions, he sold himself naturally. He didn't have to pretend that he enjoyed what he was doing or that he liked being around the gamblers and high-rollers. He had the advantage of genuinely loving his jobs, and his bosses and customers responded positively to him. No matter what he was assigned to do, he never complained. When people told him they needed him to work on a night he had scheduled off, he would always say, "I'll be there." In turn, he had no problem asking people for help when he needed it, since he had done them many favors in the past.

Dino understood how selling worked in this environment, and he enjoyed the process. He also understood the importance of relationships and networking in the gaming business, so when he was a floor boss and David Hilton, Baron's son, was working in the pit, Dino made an effort to help him learn the ropes. Dino's true forte, though, was running golf, blackjack, craps, and other special-event tournaments. He made a name for himself first at the Flamingo and then at the Venetian, and he has probably brought in more customers through these events than anyone in the history of Las Vegas. His ability to pull these events off, combined with his energy and love for the scene itself, makes him a great salesperson.

I'll tell you more about Dino in the next chapter, but for now try to keep in mind how you appear to a buyer when you're trying to convince him of something. Try to see yourself through the eyes of your boss or a prospective customer when you are making an argument or pitching an idea. Did you come off as sincere? Were you advocating a position you truly believed in? Did you feel comfortable and natural with how you were selling? Next time you try to make a sale, think about these questions immediately afterward and determine whether you can answer yes to all of them.

CHAPTER 8

GO WHERE THE STARS AREN'T

Most people want glamour jobs. If you're in business, you want to work for General Motors or a similarly well-known corporation. If you're a lawyer, you hope to join the biggest legal firm in town. If you're a consultant, you set your sights on McKinsey. If you're a banker, you want a job with Chase or some other top financial services empire. More than that, people dream about huge starting salaries, great perks, impressive-sounding titles, and finding a position that offers a fast track to the top.

All this is human nature, and if you can find one of these positions and thrive in it, more power to you. Realistically, though, C students aren't likely to receive offers from the best companies for the best positions when they're starting out. If you aren't as polished and presentable as the next person, if you are a woman attempting to make it in a male-dominated industry, if you have had some false career starts, or if you went to an average school, you are in a one-down position. Even if you secure a great job at a top company in your field, you're going to be competing against peers with more natural advantages than you possess. Management is likely to favor the Yale graduate or the A student with the photographic memory, at least in the initial career stages.

I'm not trying to discourage you from pursuing your dream job. One of the messages of this book is that persistence, gumption, and street smarts pay off, and you may beat the odds and become successful at the leading company in your industry. My advice, though, is to temper your dream with reality when necessary. Don't waste years trying to get a job at company A when they keep slamming the door in your face or stay with company A when it becomes clear you're not the sort of person who rises very high in their organization.

Recognize that you have more options than you may think. If you doubt this last statement, consider the careers of the high achievers you've met in these pages.

CAREER PATH OPTIONS

I began as a trainee at a large Pittsburgh food company, moved to a midsize Chicago ad agency, worked for a small entrepreneurial direct marketer, and then found my spot at a small ad agency and grew with them over the next thirty years.

Art Frigo started at 3M, went back to school to gain more skills, worked for a consultant, took a corporate job at one of the consulting firm's clients, and then launched his career as an entrepreneur and ran a variety of highly successful companies.

Louise O'Sullivan started as a teacher and became the CEO of a foodservice equipment manufacturer.

Larry Levy started in real estate, opened a restaurant, and eventually created a new type of company that provides food catering for sports and entertainment venues.

Mike Waters and Richard Donchin joined family businesses and eventually remade them in their own images.

Sam Morasca worked at Shell his entire career.

I mention these different career paths again to remind you that there is more than one road to success. Each of us found our paths in our own ways, sometimes after taking detours or hitting dead ends. Even though we may have made mistakes, we instinctively recognized when we found something that was right for us. The first step in recognizing the path that suits you is being aware of the various types of work environments and how you might fit in. Consider the following six possibilities:

1. BIG CORPORATIONS/LEADING COMPANIES IN FIELD.

These huge companies are exciting, dynamic places in which to work and offer opportunities smaller companies may lack, including the chance to work in foreign offices, rotate through a variety of jobs, and compete with some of the best and brightest minds in a given field. On the negative side, these organizations often have cutthroat cultures and can make mincemeat of C students and others who aren't ready for an ultra-competitive environment. It is easy to get lost and stuck in large companies, and bureaucratic red tape can be frustrating for people who like to get things done quickly. Politics are often part of these cultures, and the people who succeed know how to play the game. In some of these corporations people reach the management level by working an old boys' network. If you lack the pedigree to be included in this network it will be more difficult to reach your career goals.

2. SMALLER, ENTREPRENEURIAL COMPANIES.

In most entrepreneurial environments what counts most is what you can contribute. Management tends to discount background—schools, grade point averages, ethnicity, gender, and so on—in favor of performance. People will give you a chance to prove yourself here, but be prepared for long hours and challenging work. Software firms are an example of this type of company, and they often are dynamic, exciting places in which to work, but they can also be volatile places where the workforce can be cut dramatically or the entire company can go under with the loss of a single customer. You need to determine if a risk-taking, fast-moving, open culture fits who you are.

3. FAMILY BUSINESSES OR FAMILYLIKE CULTURES.

C students often benefit from nurturing environments, and family-run companies or cultures that treat employees like family may be a good place for you. You may be the type of person who learns best when bosses are patient and supportive and your colleagues cooperate rather than compete. Family businesses have downsides, though. As in a family, the patriarch or matriarch can play favorites, and if it is a true family business, the sons and daughters of the people who run the business will receive the top positions. Family businesses can also be idiosyncratic places where issues aren't always handled professionally or in a consistent manner.

4. PROFESSIONAL SERVICE FIRMS.

Law firms, public relations firms, financial services companies, ad agencies, and consulting firms are common types. Professional service firms are usually meritocracies, more so than product-based companies. This is great for C students, who receive more opportunities to prove themselves. If you like working with other professionals and providing a specialized service to potentially demanding clients, this may be a good place for you. Major differences exist between the practice of law and public relations, for instance. Nonetheless, most firms, regardless of their particular area of expertise, are intellectually challenging, people-oriented places, and being a good relationship builder is often a more valuable skill than being brilliantly analytical. The largest firms in each area, however, tend to resemble the largest corporations: They place a high value on where you went to school and other aspects of your background. Professional service firms can also reward the "grinds"—people willing to work around the clock for their firms. Junior members of management consultant firms and associates at law firms are especially vulnerable to this workaholic syndrome.

5. SOLE PROPRIETORSHIPS/OWN BUSINESS.

In theory, being your own boss is an ideal situation for C students. In reality, it's not always feasible. As I told my son, the best time to go into business for yourself is early in your career when you aren't responsible for a spouse or children and don't have a large mortgage payment or a house to maintain. When you're young, you have the time and freedom to devote to your business, and the consequences of the business failing aren't as serious as they are when you are supporting a family. Of course, many younger people lack the financial wherewithal to start their own businesses in the first place. In addition, not all C students are cut out for being in business for themselves. It can be a lonely experience, and not everyone wants to take on the multiple tasks that being your own boss entails. If you're not certain you want to have your own business—or you lack the financial means to do so—it makes sense to work for someone else initially to get a feel for that environment.

6. NOT-FOR-PROFIT ASSOCIATIONS.

C students with high emotional intelligence often feel comfortable working for not-for-profits. They want to make a difference in the world rather than a profit, and these associations give them that opportunity. While the salaries usually aren't as high as in the for-profit world, these associations often offer generous benefits. Their cultures tend to be more humanistic than those in the for-profit sector, and many of these associations are highly professional and well-run. The ability to empathize with the plight of the groups these associations serve is prized, and C students who are passionate about specific causes can flourish in not-for-profits. At the same time, some not-for-profits are surprisingly political, and people fight and maneuver to get ahead with the same ferocity as in the corporate universe. Be aware, too, that not-for-profits can impose restrictions and regulations on their people to the point that you can feel hamstrung. If you hate bureaucracy and paperwork, this may not be the best place for you.

These six categories aren't the only ones, and in some instances you'll find hybrids—the entrepreneurial corporation, for example, or the family-run professional service firm. But these six categories can help you to start thinking about which types appeal to you and which ones you find not to your liking. Too often C students are so grateful for any job offers they receive that they'll accept one without considering the environment. Recognize that you have options, and that you should at least determine in advance which ones make sense for you.

HOW TO GET IN THE DOOR AND WHAT TO DO ONCE YOU'RE IN

Perhaps you've applied for jobs advertised in trade publications or online services and never heard back. It may be that you've actually gone on interviews but have left feeling you didn't make a good impression—or maybe you feel you presented yourself well but you weren't called back for a second interview. After the rejections accumulate, you start asking yourself, "What am I doing wrong?"

The answer may be that you're a C student attempting to get a job like an A student. You can't just present your résumé or yourself in an interview and expect to receive job offers. No doubt you're an interesting person who has done well in certain areas of your life. Imagine, though, if the person who interviews before you is an Eagle Scout, an Ivy League school graduate who had perfect scores on his SATs, did a summer internship with the most prestigious company in your industry, and has recommendations from three CEOs who all play golf with his father. I'm exaggerating, but I'm sure you get my point: You're not only fighting a numbers game to get in the door, you're waging an uphill battle to obtain more notice than all the other well-qualified candidates vying for the job.

Fortunately, you have resources and options, no matter what your grade point average might have been. Specifically, here are four ways you can secure interviews and make a strong impression:

1. APPLY FOR JOBS ONE POSITION REMOVED FROM THE ONE YOU REALLY WANT.

As I've mentioned, I applied for ad agency jobs and took one in the account group, not because I wanted to be an account executive but because I saw it as a way to secure a job as a producer eventually. Though my career aspirations were misplaced, my strategy was sound. Creative jobs at ad agencies are in high demand, and the easiest way to get one may be through a sideways move rather than directly applying for a particular job. By interviewing for an account or media position, you get in the door, establish relationships, and give yourself an edge over outsiders to obtain a creative position.

This same philosophy works in most fields. Louise O'Sullivan started her business career writing technical case histories, and only after putting in her time did she receive an opportunity to get into sales. Art Frigo was working for a corporation when he seized the opportunity to create one of the first leveraged buyouts in this country. Dino Child's entire early career has been a progression of applying for one job to gain leverage on another. He moved from Las Vegas busboy to server, dealer, pit boss, floor boss, and operations to marketing; he started in the restaurant and golf areas and found ways to find a place for himself in the gaming areas he loves.

The big obstacle for many C students is moving from the outside to the inside, since once you're part of an organization all sorts of doors can open. I'm not advocating applying to be the custodian of a NASA building because you want to be an astronaut. People who start in the mailroom often end up in the mailroom. Contrary to the myth, not many top executives work their way up from such humble beginnings. Therefore, be astute about the jobs that are only one department or level removed from the ones you really want.

2. TRANSLATE SOMETHING YOU KNOW OR HAVE DONE INTO A JOB INTERVIEW ASSET.

It would be nice if you had an internship with Tom Peters under your belt when you applied for that assistant brand manager job at a Fortune 100 company, but the odds are you don't have that credential on your résumé. In fact, you may not have any singular job or educational experience that will separate you from a hundred other candidates. On the other hand, you probably possess some experience—job or otherwise—that you can use to your advantage.

If you recall, I used my experience selling baby food for Heinz to convince the Edward H. Weiss ad agency that I knew what it took to secure shelf space, a concern their Wish-Bone client had. Mostly, I knew how to stack baby food on the shelves, but that wasn't the point. I had real experience in an area relevant to one of their major clients, and I used it to make the agency believe they needed me. When an interviewer thinks, "We need this person," you've got the job.

If you haven't had the relevant job experience to make you a strong candidate for a position, consider what part-time or summer work you've done that might give you a leg up on the job. Maybe you coordinated social activities for your college sorority, and you're applying for an events planning position. Perhaps you worked as a camp counselor, and you're trying to land a human resources job where you'll need to use some of the same people skills. If you were the captain of your soccer team or the president of the debate society, you can make a good case for your leadership potential.

My first major hire at Eicoff was Rick Sangerman. I interviewed many people for the account executive position; some of them had significant agency experience, but Rick had none. Rick, though, had been a tennis pro at a club in one of Chicago's affluent suburbs. When he told me of his challenging experiences as a tennis pro, I figured if he could teach demanding suburban matrons to play tennis at eight A.M., he could handle ad agency clients.

Becky Jewett was a student guide in college; one time, the father of a potential student she was taking on a tour said, "See if you can convince my daughter to go here." Becky succeeded, and later she applied for a job at this man's company. He remembered her, gave her a job, helped her capitalize on career opportunities, and became her first mentor.

You should also do some research prior to your job interview. This may sound obvious, but I can't tell you how many people have walked into my office and couldn't name a single Eicoff client. I've taken the time to read this person's résumé; the least the interviewee can do is read a little about the agency. More than that, though, you should read and think about some of the issues facing the company where you want to get a job or the largest questions confronting their industry. Nothing impresses me more than when job candidates express an educated point of view. In other words, they share a perspective on a problem or opportunity facing our business that demonstrates they've done their home-work. Even if their point of view is naive or just plain wrong, they still get points for making the effort and showing a willingness to express an opinion.

3. BE CONFIDENT, HUMBLE, AND YOURSELF.

Don't try to be something you're not. Don't walk into an interview and act the part you think will impress the interviewer. Most people will see through your act, and you'll be hard-pressed to maintain the role you've created if you're actually hired. As I've stated earlier, people respond to authenticity. This doesn't mean you should be overly casual or feel free to say anything that pops into your head. Instead, recognize that you're engaged in a formal interview and be yourself within this context.

No matter who you are, you should strive for the middle ground between confidence and humility. People who are overly confident may strike interviewers as arrogant. After all, an interviewer will think, "What has this person accomplished that justi-fies such an attitude?" Similarly, people who are overly shy or self-deprecating come off as weak and uncertain. While everyone wants to hire someone who is nice, no one wants to hire someone who is fragile. Most jobs require initiative and aggressive pursuit of goals, and if a candidate gives the appearance of being too meek and mild to do anything but follow orders, she probably won't get the job.

Perhaps the biggest mistake a C student can make is to adopt an arrogant attitude. Some C students have an image in their minds of what the best job candidates look like. They envision a superior attitude, an unshakable certainty that they know all the answers, and an unwillingness to admit a mistake. Perhaps some interviewers and companies are looking for arrogance in job candidates, but this quality turns off most people. I remember when a major college football player applied for a job at our agency. Not only was he big, handsome, and had a 4.0 grade point average, he walked in the door like he owned the place. When I talked to him a few days later and told him we had chosen someone else for the job, he was incredulous. He kept repeating, "I had a 4.0. How much better can you get?" This smart football player made a good impression until he opened his mouth. We, like many companies, don't have a culture of arrogance, and so despite his intelligence and accomplishments on the football field, he would not have fit in.

4. RECOGNIZE THAT INFORMATIONAL INTERVIEWS CAN BE MORE THAN INFORMATIONAL.

Don't turn up your nose at interviews that seem to hold little prospect of a job offer. I understand that after weeks or months of fruitless searching, the last thing you want to do is get dressed up and endure a trip to an office where there seems to be no prospect of employment. You might think that you already have all the information about a job or an industry that you need, and an informational interview sounds like a waste of time.

It isn't. Yes, people may make it clear to you that they don't have a job to offer, but that doesn't mean they won't have job in the future or that they won't steer you toward a friend or former colleague who does have an opening. It may be that some informational interviews don't lead anywhere or enlighten you in any way, but you have to go to them or you won't happen upon the ones that do lead somewhere or offer enlightenment. In fact, if you go to ten informational interviews, I would bet that at least five of them will prove useful.

Cara, for instance, graduated in the middle of the pack from a fair-to-middling law school and was trying to land a job at one of Chicago's major law firms. Despite her persistence, no one would hire her. In almost all her interviews, Cara heard the same thing: She needed to have been law review at her school or have gone to one of the top schools to merit consideration. A friend of a friend eventually arranged for Cara to have an informational interview at one of the few major law firms she hadn't visited. The partner who interviewed her, Laura, started the interview by reiterating to Cara what she had told her on the phone: The firm had filled all their openings and they didn't expect to be hiring again for at least another six months. Laura gave her standard talk about the history of the firm, its culture, and so on. Cara asked a number of standard questions. Then Laura glanced at Cara's résumé and noticed that she listed tae kwon do as a hobby. It turned out that Laura had just started taking lessons at a dojo in her neighborhood, and Cara had been taking lessons for years and was a black belt. The next half hour of the informational interview was focused on the martial arts. Two weeks later Laura heard about an opening for an associate at another major law firm and immediately called Cara to ask her if she was interested. Cara was indeed interested, Laura recommended her to the attorney doing the hiring, and Cara was selected for the position.

Be aware, too, that the more interviews you go on, the more likely you are to encounter a fellow C student. There are more of us than there are of any other group, and it may be that your interviewer will recognize something in you that he remembers in himself. It may be that you, like your interviewer, made a few false career starts. It's possible that your career goals are extraordinarily ambitious, especially given your background, and the person with whom you're interviewing had the same overly ambitious approach early in his career. Whatever the reason, if someone resonates to who you are and what you hope to accomplish, he is likely to help you with information, contacts, or even a job offer.

I know many successful people of my generation who have vowed to return favors done for them years ago. For instance, when I arrived in Chicago from Pittsburgh, I went on an informational interview with George Rink, president of a small ad agency called Rink Wells. I was ushered into his office, and when we sat down, he said, "I'm going to help you find a job, but I need to extract a promise from you."

Excited that he was going to help me but wary of what he might request, I asked him what he wanted me to do.

"Later in your career, when someone knocks on your door and comes looking for a job, you'll help them."

I agreed, and I've kept that promise.

THE VACUUM PRINCIPLE

According to Art Frigo, the vacuum principle should guide C students in their job choices. Art says that some organizations are missing people with key skills and knowledge; there is a talent vacuum in these companies, providing opportunities for perceptive job seekers. Generally these are smaller or midsize companies rather than the largest ones, and the competition for both entry-level jobs and advancement isn't as fierce as in the best-known companies. If someone who is great at building customer relationships emerges, who is savvy about financial issues, or who is a great innovator, she will be recognized quickly and rewarded. In other words, it is much easier to stand out in a vacuum than in a crowded field.

Top companies are great places for some people. If you are one of the chosen few and become a star at IBM or General Motors, you will be well compensated, receive wonderful perks, and enjoy the prestige of working for a world-renowned organization. If, however, you are not a star at these companies, you can easily become lost in the shuffle, you will be vulnerable to the next downsizing, and your talents can be overlooked easily.

Therefore, be alert for openings at companies where there are vacuums. Many of the people profiled in these pages found such opportunities. When Norm Bobins left American National Bank to go to the smaller Exchange National Bank, he was leaving to go to a place where he could shine. Exchange clearly needed someone with his talents, and as a result his opportunities there were greater than at the larger American National.

Finding a company with a vacuum can be tricky, since a vacuum for one person might not be a vacuum for another. For instance, you may be an information system wizard, but a small software company may be filled with information technology geniuses. An old-line manufacturing company, however, may have an IT vacuum that you can fill. Ideally, what you're looking for is a company that needs what you have to offer. To help determine whether a company fits this description, ask the following questions:

- Does the organization seem to be overstaffed? Are employees always fighting to work on choice projects? Does it seem like there aren't enough good projects to go around? Do people complain about being stuck in positions or not having the chance to show what they can do?

- Are your knowledge and skills significantly different from those possessed by most employees? Do you have a particular talent that is particularly valuable to the company right now, one that they have found to be in short supply? Do you see your talent growing in value to the company based on emerging trends and changing market conditions?

WORKING FOR YOURSELF VERSUS WORKING FOR SOMEONE ELSE

As I'm sure you've noticed, many of the people profiled in these pages are entrepreneurs. Some started their own businesses early in their careers while others did so only after spending years working for someone else. For C students, entrepreneurship is always an option worth considering. When you are your own boss, you free yourself from the prejudices of bosses and anti-C-student cultures. It is difficult to imagine people like Rich Melman and Mike Krasny working for anyone but themselves. These are people with strong visions who probably would never have fulfilled their potential working for large organizations. At the same time, individuals such as Sam Morasca, Louise O'Sullivan, and Dino Child have flourished working for others. They found the right environments for their particular talents, and it didn't matter that some of them lacked sterling academic credentials and others didn't fit the business executive norm.

You may be at a point where you're contemplating this decision, and if so, circumstance may dictate what you do next. For instance, you may be young and unencumbered, have some money from an inheritance or some other source, and the freedom to take a risk with your own business right now. On the other hand, you may have to postpone your entrepreneurial dream for five or ten years because you married and had a family right after you graduated and you need a more stable income than your own business can afford. Many entrepreneurs pay their dues working for large organizations, acquiring the skills, capital, and contacts necessary to go out on their own. I also know some people who tried to be entrepreneurs and realized that the dream was much better than the reality; they missed the resources large organizations could provide and found the entrepreneurial risks too stressful.

My experiences have taught me that some people are constitutionally unable to work for others. Al Eicoff, for instance, would have been a bull in any organization's china shop. Headstrong, intolerant of bureaucracy, and inflexible, he would have been miserable at any large corporation. Dennis Bookshester, on the other hand, relished the responsibilities that came with working in a hierarchical organization. At Burdines, Carson Pine Scott, and other companies, he quickly mastered how to use a large company's many resources to achieve ambitious goals.

While there is no certain way to know whether you are an entrepreneur or an organizational type besides trying these roles out, thinking about the type of student you were can give you a clue about where you'll fit in best. Some C students were highly social and relationship-oriented, while others were loners who pursued one area of interest and ignored other subjects. The former tend to do well in organizations and the latter as entrepreneurs. Granted, this is a broad generalization, but think about which traits from your academic past best describe you. As a student, you:

- Enjoyed going to parties and engaging in other social activities more than studying.

- Were a member of a fraternity or sorority.

- Served on various committees such as the student council, Greek rush, and so on.

- Played on a sports team.

- Received your best grades in classes that were highly structured and placed significant weight on class participation and team projects.

Or you:

- Had a particular subject (not necessarily an academic one) that fascinated you to the point that it dominated your time.

- Rarely participated in class or, at the other extreme, tended to express opinions with great passion and without concern for how others would react.

- Sometimes wrote papers that ignored the topic that was assigned.

- Ignored most school-sponsored activities unless they had to do with the subject that fascinated you.

- Sometimes got in trouble for violating school rules and policies.

Clearly, the former list is more indicative of an organizational person and the latter of an entrepreneur.

KNOW WHEN IT'S TIME TO LEAVE

Some C students stay too long at their jobs. They are so grateful to be employed that they are afraid to look for other positions. They convince themselves that "this is the best I can do" and remain with the same company even though they might be bored out of their minds. They may even rationalize away their boredom, convincing themselves that everyone goes through career phases in which they aren't particularly excited by their work and that putting in their time now will pay dividends in the future.

Perhaps. More likely, though, the boredom will make it that much more difficult to achieve your career goals. If you're bored and unchallenged, you can't succeed. If you dread getting up in the morning and going to work, you're in the wrong environment. Inertia kills careers, and it kills C students' careers more easily than others. In your first ten years after school you should be testing yourself and exploring different possibilities. You may be able to test and explore in one company that offers you all sorts of challenges. Many of you, though, are going to have to move around a bit, and a sure sign that you should move is when you are bored for a sustained period of time.

To gauge your degree of boredom, ask yourself the following questions regularly:

- Have I learned something new this week?

- Do I need to stretch to master a new skill or execute an assignment?

- Am I forming and strengthening relationships that are helping me build a professional network?

- Do I feel like an A student in my job (top of my class, achievement-oriented, excelling at what I do, looking forward to the next assignment) or a C student (average, just trying to get things in on time, indifferent to the next assignment)?

You should also leave an average job when above-average opportunities present themselves. Norm Bobins, Dennis Bookshester, and Becky Jewett all left better-than-average jobs for great ones. They recognized that they needed to take a chance in order to succeed at a higher level than was possible at their current jobs. Their opportunities weren't necessarily for more money (though that came to them as a consequence of their achievements) but for more responsibility and more challenging goals.

I'm not telling you to change jobs at the drop of a hat. I've been at the same place for over thirty-five years, so clearly I believe that if you find a great situation you should make the most of it. Just don't fool yourself into believing it's great when it's really just safe and secure. Above all else, look at the company and determine whether you think it will give you a fair chance to be a star or if it's crowded with stars who are nothing at all like you. If the latter is true, it's going to be tough for you to do well. If, however, you see a company that's looking hard for someone to come in and become the star they desperately need, grab that job and shine.

CHAPTER 9

BE A SMART RISK-TAKER

Taking risks can give you an edge over people who possess more education and better credentials than you do. Many A students play it safe because they don't have to take chances to advance in their careers. They are on the fast track from the start, and as long as they do what is expected of them, they'll achieve certain career goals.

You don't have to take wild risks or do anything crazy, but you need to be willing to put your pride, your knowledge, and even your job on the line at some point. You might have to risk embarrassment by telling your boss you don't understand. You might have to risk failure by taking on a challenging assignment that you're not certain you can complete successfully. You might have to risk losing money by starting your own business or by taking a new job that pays less than you want but gives you the chance to grow professionally. In other words, you should be willing to lose anything from a little pride to a small amount of money in the short run for a bigger gain down the road.

C students shouldn't be afraid of risk, but they should be smart about it. All of us have different tolerance levels for risk. You need to know your risk profile and use it to get ahead. First, though, let me give you a better sense of why C students should take risks.

THE LINK BETWEEN RISK AND REWARD

If Rich Melman had stayed in the family business, he might be running a nice little delicatessen in Skokie today. If Richard Donchin had been content to operate one profitable hardware store, he might never have taken the chances necessary to build a success-ful chain. If Mike Krasny had been satisfied selling computers di-rectly to a small target market, he would never have built CDW into a mammoth, multimarket business.

Each of these individuals took risks that were right for them. By taking these risks, they gained a competitive edge in their ca-reers and businesses that they couldn't have obtained any other way. Rich Melman's daring originality in his restaurant concepts helped him become an enormous success. If he had chosen safer, more traditional concepts, he might still have been successful, but on a much smaller scale. Each time he launches a restaurant with an unusual or provocative theme he takes the chance of being ridiculed, not to mention losing a lot of money. Instead, his groundbreaking restaurants have brought him national fame.

At the same time, Rich never took foolish risks. He always did his homework beforehand, launched concepts that he was pas-sionate about, and created a business model that helped him in-crease the odds of success for each restaurant he opened. Buoyed by his success, Rich could have embarked on a far riskier course and opened more places with less research and passion. Instead, he stayed within his risk profile.

I have always tried to do the same thing. People have won-dered why I never opened my own ad agency, as I certainly had opportunities to do so. The rewards for starting my own agency, though, never outweighed the risks. Not only was I generously compensated, but Ogilvy & Mather gave (and continues to give)

Eicoff a tremendous amount of independence. I never was one to risk everything on one roll of the dice. At the same time, I also recognized that if I didn't take risks, I would never achieve my goals.

About fifteen years ago, our agency was at a crossroads. We needed to improve our creative—the production and conceptual quality of our commercials—if we were to attract more Fortune 500 clients. We saw a tremendous opportunity to expand our client base, since at the time larger advertisers were just starting to grasp the potential of television direct-response advertising. We needed to demonstrate that our commercials not only could produce results but would build and maintain our clients' brands. To me, this meant we needed to hire a creative department head from the outside. We had always selected this position from within the agency, believing that it takes time to master the nuances of a television direct-response commercial, and that someone from a general agency background would struggle. I also knew that some creative department veterans would resent an outsider becoming their boss.

I made the decision that these risks were worth taking. I hired Sandy Stern, who had been a top creative director at agencies such as Foote, Cone & Belding and J. Walter Thompson and had won a Cannes Gold Lion for her work. It was the single best hire I ever made. She was a quick study and figured out the nuances of television direct response faster than I could have hoped. More important, she had a vision of what our creative could become and made it happen. She not only inspired the creative department to attain a higher standard, she also brought in other creative people who could achieve this standard.

Perhaps I would not have taken this risk if I had been a CEO at a large mainstream agency. But as a C student I understood that at certain times you have to take chances to move to the next level. No one is going to give you anything. You have to swallow hard and take the risk.

Risks come in all shapes and sizes. To help you prepare yourself to take the right ones, let's look at the range of risks you will face in your career.

FROM SPEAKING UP TO MOVING ON

Before you determine your risk profile, you'll need to familiarize yourself with all the kinds of risks you're likely to face over time. In the following pages I describe six of the most common types of risks, from the small risks, where not so much is at stake, to the big risks, where everything is at stake.

1. ASK FOR HELP.

This might be the smallest risk, but it can feel like a big one when you're starting out at a job and need to go into your boss's or even a colleague's office and say "I don't understand." You're risking that these people will think you're dumb or slow. In reality, they will probably be glad to help, but in your mind you might feel that you're exposing your ignorance.

As uncomfortable as this risk can be, it's absolutely essential for learning. The reward is knowledge, exactly what you need to get your career off the ground. It's fine to try to figure things out for yourself, but when you become stuck on a major project or feel like you're getting yourself in trouble, ask for advice. By doing so, not only do you gain knowledge but you establish productive relationships with peers and potential mentors.

To make it easier for you to take this risk, keep the following truism in mind:

Know what you know as well as what you don't know.

2. EXPRESS A DIFFERENT OPINION.

At some point while you're sitting in a meeting or talking with your boss you'll realize your ideas run counter to the conventional wisdom. Do you articulate these ideas? Well, it depends on the situation. For instance, if you're meeting with your company's largest customer for the first time and that customer talks about the need for the company to provide faster service, you probably don't want to tell him that you believe the service is as fast as it can get. The risk here far exceeds the reward. On the other hand, you may feel so strongly about a subject that you'll risk disapproval to make your ideas known.

Be aware that if you consistently express contrary opinions, you'll develop a reputation as a contrarian. This will not help your career, since you'll be viewed as someone who creates conflict rather than consensus, who puts the kibosh on promising projects. If, however, you pick your spots carefully, you'll gain the reputation of being someone who isn't afraid to speak his mind. The risk of occasionally being rejected or censured is worth it if you build this reputation.

3. VOLUNTEER FOR A CHALLENGING PROJECT.

Earlier I talked about the value of raising your hand, but now let's look at the risks associated with volunteering. Taking on a tough project means risking failure. If you have a C-student mentality, you may be reluctant to risk failure. You may believe it's better to stick with projects you know you can handle than sign up for extra credit. In many cases, though, these projects are can't-lose propositions. Even if the project falls short of expectations, you'll be given points for trying (assuming you turned in a good effort). If the project succeeds, you'll be a hero. Remember how

Louise O'Sullivan took the chance of going on the road with her company's sales representatives? She had little experience in the field, but she saw the opportunity to make a difference. Louise accepted this challenging assignment and impressed everyone, including her company's sales reps, with her insights and suggestions.

On the other hand, no one likes signing up for a doomed mission. When I say "challenging project," I mean one that has at least the possibility of success. It may also offer you the opportunity to display your knowledge and skills to a wider audience; your boss's boss may not realize what a good numbers guy you are or how savvy you are about the manufacturing processes.

4. MAKE A TOUGH DECISION THAT NOT EVERYONE AGREES WITH.

Here the risk involves offending or alienating people. You may decide to hire someone who is your boss's third choice for the job or fire someone he favors. You may decide to replace an outmoded software system with a new one, recognizing that there's going to be grumbling about having to learn an unfamiliar system. You may choose a higher-cost supplier that you feel will provide better service, knowing that you're going to take flack from the budget-conscious.

You can't please all the people all the time. In fact, it's much better to develop a reputation for being decisive than for being a pleaser. If you want to move up in any organization, you're going to deal with increasingly tougher decisions at each level, and you may make some enemies as a result of your choices. When you're confronted with tough decisions, make them based on your beliefs rather than on political considerations.

5. ACCEPT A NEW POSITION THAT REQUIRES A STRETCH.

The risk, of course, is that you'll fall flat on your face. The reward is that you'll learn and grow. As I've mentioned, I didn't know anything about getting new business when I took the job at Eicoff as the person in charge of new business. Mike Krasny started his direct-sales computer business without experience in direct marketing. Sam Morasca took on the job of running a chemical plant without the technical expertise to do so.

Here, there's a real risk that you can make mistakes in the spotlight. These mistakes might even hurt your career temporarily. Consider, though, the upside. Stretch assignments force you out of your comfort zone. You have to learn new skills and gain new knowledge, and though this can be an uncomfortable process, you can emerge with a more marketable profile.

You don't want to take stretch assignments that will stretch you so hard that you'll snap. Like a college basketball star, you need to assess whether you're ready to leave school for the NBA or if another year of college experience will increase your odds of success at the pro level. The best stretch assignments are the ones where you have at least 50 percent of the experience and expertise for a job, but not all. If you know enough and possess sufficient talent, you will be in a good position to learn on the job and get up to speed before you fall flat on your face.

6. LEAVE A GOOD JOB FOR A POTENTIALLY GREAT OPPORTUNITY.

This risk here is that the great opportunity won't work out. Kathryn, for instance, was a newspaper publishing executive in charge of advertising and sales for a major daily. She knew that if she remained with her newspaper, she would never have a chance to be publisher. In the newspaper's history, neither the publisher nor the associate publisher had ever been a woman. On top of that, the people on the newspaper's business side who got the top spots tended to fit a certain profile: a golfer, a member of an exclusive suburban club, an ability to fit in easily at any gathering and charm people. Kathryn was a graduate of a state college, the only daughter of parents who had worked in factories. Not only didn't she golf or make small talk easily, but her husband was a stay-at-home-dad who took care of their three kids. When she was offered the job of publisher at a smaller magazine, she knew she was risking a secure, well-paying job for a top title in a more volatile environment, but she took it. After a year, though, the publication was in serious financial trouble—the owners had not been honest when they hired her. Though the risk didn't pan out in the short term, it eventually helped her secure a publisher job two years later. The experience of being a publisher for one year gave her the credentials and knowledge she needed to be a strong candidate for the position.

Seemingly great opportunities can include everything from the chance to start your own business to a job for more money with more responsibility at another organization. These opportunities don't come along often, and when they do, you should consider them seriously even if they may entail significant risk. It's difficult to leave a place where you've worked for fifteen years and have a job for life if you want it. Risking your life savings on a new business is even more scary. Recognize, though, that you can reduce these risks, at least to some extent, based on *how* you leave. Some people leave on good terms, making sure their employer knows how much they appreciate what they've learned and how it has helped them. Others, though, burn their bridges. I once had an executive who came into my office, said he had another job offer, and demanded to be made a senior vice president or he would leave. I told him, "There's the door." He departed on bad terms and increased that risk.

Likewise, when you depart on good terms, if things don't work out, there's more of a chance your former employer will take you back. Even if they don't, however, they are more likely to give you good recommendations and keep you informed when they hear about jobs at other companies.

WHAT'S YOUR RISK PROFILE?

Not all C students have the same tolerance for risk. If you think about risk as a continuum, at one end you have someone like Flip who relishes high risk levels, and at the other end you have people who rarely take even the smallest risks of asking for help or expressing a different opinion. You need to locate yourself on this continuum so you can develop a feel for which types of risks you should take. Before helping you make this assessment, I'd like to share two stories of risk-taking, the first of which requires an extremely high tolerance, the second of which requires an average or slightly above average amount.

Rich Melman's first restaurant was R.J. Grunts, located in Chicago's Lincoln Park area. When he opened R.J. Grunts in 1971, his vision involved not only the food but the music they played, the attitude and look of the servers, and the decor. Everything was geared to twentysomethings, and this emphasis on hip food and ambiance was unique at the time. Rich was twenty-eight when he opened R.J. Grunts, and he sank all the money he had into the restaurant: He put in $10,000, and his partner put in $7,000. During the restaurant's first week of operation, the place did $2,000 in sales, but the payroll was also $2,000.

"I had no one to turn to if it didn't work; my parents weren't wealthy," Rich said. "I was living in a two-hundred-dollar-a-month apartment, I was working sixteen or seventeen hours a day, and I ate all my meals at the restaurant. I kept trying to pump myself up, but I was getting nervous because after two and a half months, nothing was happening. I remember going home on a Wednesday during this period, and I was more depressed than any time before or since, except for when my dad and my best friend died. I had tried every idea I thought would work to get the restaurant going, and I had failed. I owed forty thousand dollars by this time, and I figured I'd have to fold the restaurant, get two jobs, and then in about six years I could pay off my debt. After taking a shower, I went back to the restaurant and told my partner I had failed, but he didn't accept it and told me everyone was talking about the place. I didn't see that translating into income.

"Then someone stopped by Grunts who wanted to take me to a restaurant where they did a great Dungeness crab, so I went out there with him. I got back to R.J. Grunts later that night and there were people waiting in line! We'd never had a night before this when there were more than twenty-five people there at any one time. The place was up for grabs. I tore off my sport coat and went to work in the kitchen, and from that night on, everything clicked."

Could you tolerate the high level of risk that Rich operated under early in his career? Would you be willing to spend the next six years trying to work off your debt if your risk didn't pan out? Be aware, too, that your risk profile changes over time. Typically as you enter middle age and achieve a certain level of success, your tolerance for risk decreases. In fact, Rich says that today when he opens a new restaurant, "I don't take a lot of chances; I want the odds in my favor." He explains that those first two and half months with R.J. Grunts were a cautionary experience.

"People talk about the Great Depression and how they were changed forever. That [the early days with Grunts] was my 'Great Depression.'"

Now let's look at another level of risk tolerance. When Richard Donchin was twenty-eight, he had been out on his own for a while but had decided to rejoin his father and help him run his hardware store. It quickly became apparent that they needed to expand, especially when the Handy Andy chain announced plans to open a location only six blocks from their store. Richard proposed to his father that they open a store seven times larger than their original one, and his father agreed.

"I had an entrepreneurial spirit," Richard said. "I wasn't afraid to put inventory in. At the beginning, my father and I just took living expenses, no salary. We kept the money in the business, and we were always short of money because our sales were booming and we needed inventory. When Handy Andy came in and we decided to open the second store, it didn't scare me. I had confidence in myself and in our people that we could make it work. There is always a risk in opening a new store, and each time we've opened a new one over the years, that risk always exists. But each time it was a bit easier because we practiced doing it. It was like a golf swing in that it was repeatable."

Now assess your risk profile by making a check mark next to the following statements that apply to you:

___ I would gladly risk every penny I've saved for the chance to start my own business.

___ I have no problem giving up a job where I'm well paid and respected for a better job.

__ I am a risk-taker by nature and engage in outdoor activities such as mountain climbing, parachute jumping, whitewater rafting, and other sports with an element of danger.

__ I enjoy gambling in Vegas and playing card games with friends and have no problem when the stakes are high.

__ I frequently ask for help at work when I don't know what to do.

__ I don't think twice about saying what I believe, and I don't care if it runs counter to what my boss or anyone else thinks.

__ Whenever an interesting assignment comes up, I volunteer for it and don't worry about whether I'm equipped to handle it.

__ I make decisions easily, even ones where a lot is riding on what I decide.

__ I love taking on new positions where the bar for achievement is set high and I need to learn on the job.

__ When I fail, I always pick myself up, dust myself off, and am ready to tackle another project where the possibility of failure exists.

RISK PROFILE SCORING

8–10 checks: High-risk profile

4–7 checks: Medium-risk profile

0–3 checks: Low-risk profile

Recognize that this assessment is an intellectual exercise that might not translate perfectly to reality. Pay attention to your actual behavior in work situations. If you find you can't sleep nights when you're trying to decide whether to take a new job, that fact suggests more about your profile than if you had ten checks on the assessment. Similarly, if you only had a few checks but find yourself starting risky businesses with few qualms, then you're a higher profile than indicated.

Also, be aware that whatever your risk profile is now, it can change over time, especially as you accumulate assets and find yourself in a secure, well-paying job.

As I've emphasized, every C student has to take some risks to get ahead, but not every C student should take the same risks. Find the ones you're comfortable with and use them to advance your career.

RISK-REWARD ASSESSMENT: HOW TO DETERMINE WHETHER A SPECIFIC RISK IS WORTH TAKING

C students often have great instincts, and as I've emphasized earlier, trusting your gut is a good way to help with the tough decisions you'll have to make throughout your career, including ones involving risk. At times, however, you will face complex or confusing choices when you need more than your instinct to make the right choice. People like Art Frigo and Larry Levy have great business instincts, but they also are astute analysts of risks versus rewards. Before proceeding with a venture, they calculate what they have to lose versus what they have to win, and then they make their decisions accordingly. Instinct may tell them they should be in a given market or that they should go with a new supplier, but they analyze what their instinct is telling them.

Sometimes the risk-reward calculation is easy. There are times when one of our account people will tell me they have met with a prospective client who wants to spend a great deal of money, but there is a potential conflict with another company that has been our client for years. Even if the reward of taking on this new client is significant, the risk of losing an established client makes the decision clear: We have to turn down the new business.

You have dealt with similar easy-to-calculate risk-reward scenarios. When you were in college, you probably had to decide whether to take a class with a tough teacher who assigned a lot of homework. The risk was that you might not get a good grade and that your time would be consumed with homework from the class. The reward was that you might learn something that you really wanted to learn or that would help you in your career when you graduated. In some instances, you probably decided the risk was too great and decided to take another class. In other instances, you were so eager to learn what the class promised to teach that you didn't care how much you had to do.

C students should make this calculation a reflex. Too often, though, the C student's reflex involves only one side of the equation. People with relatively low self-esteem only look at the risk side, determining what they have to lose when faced with a choice. As a result, they shy away from taking any risks. Some C students, on the other hand, are so eager to succeed that they throw caution to the wind and only analyze the rewards attached to a decision; they can get themselves in trouble if they realize how much risk a given move involves.

While everyone has a different risk profile, it's always important to do a balanced assessment before making a decision. Here, we'll look at each of our six risk types from a risk-reward perspective. Each risk is followed by a reward question, then a risk question.

1. ASK FOR HELP.

- Is the information I'm seeking essential? Will it help me do an important job that has to be completed quickly?

- Will I likely be viewed as lazy if I request help in this particular instance? Will I be viewed as slow or incompetent because I can't do the project on my own?

2. EXPRESS A DIFFERENT OPINION.

- Do I have something important to say? Is my opinion likely to be viewed as thought-provoking and incisive? Will I be viewed as having the courage of my convictions?

- By expressing a contrary point of view, will I be viewed as contrary? Am I likely to offend someone when I articulate my opinion? Will my perspective seem odd and contribute to my reputation for being flaky?

3. VOLUNTEER FOR A CHALLENGING PROJECT.

- Will the project give me the opportunity to demonstrate my knowledge and skills to my boss and other executives in the organization? Do I have the time and energy to take on the challenge and do a good job?

- Is the project doomed from the start and is anyone associated with it likely to be adversely affected by its failure? Is this project likely to take me away from more important responsibilities?

4. MAKE A TOUGH DECISION THAT NOT EVERYONE AGREES WITH.

- By making the decision, will I be seen as decisive and able to deal with complex issues? Will people respect my decision even if they don't agree with it?

- Is the decision likely to offend a powerful executive in the organization or antagonize a client or customer? Are most people going to disagree with my decision?

5. ACCEPT A NEW POSITION THAT REQUIRES A STRETCH.

- Will I gain new knowledge and skills by taking this position that will help me achieve my career goals? Will taking this assignment demonstrate my willingness to take on fresh challenges in order to help the organization?

- Is the stretch beyond my capabilities? Am I going to be asked to do things that I am not prepared to do at this point in my career? Am I likely to fall on my face?

6. LEAVE A GOOD JOB FOR A POTENTIALLY GREAT OPPORTUNITY.

- Is the opportunity one that will provide me with the chance to grow as a professional in ways that I can't in my current position? Does it offer opportunities for achievement (financial, career, impact, responsibility) that aren't available in my current job?

- Does the great opportunity carry with it a high degree of financial risk? If the opportunity doesn't work out, how likely is it that I will be unemployed or find it difficult to obtain another job?

As you use these questions to calculate your risk versus reward, keep in mind that it is difficult for C students to take risks when they're stuck in a comfortable routine. At some point you may find yourself in a job that you can handle easily, working for a boss who isn't particularly demanding. You enjoy your colleagues and look forward to seeing them each day. The pay is good and you never have to work particularly hard. As pleasant as all this may be, the routine can quickly become a rut. You are so comfortable that you don't want to take a risk. You don't want to do anything to disturb the routine. This is fine if you're not ambitious. But it's possible that you might wake up from the routine ten years later and realize you missed your chance. Because you refused to take a risk and stretch your skills or tackle challenging projects, you never advanced in your career. Risks can make you feel uncomfortable temporarily, but this discomfort means that you're putting yourself in unfamiliar situations and learning new skills to handle them. Therefore, don't avoid risk just because you like feeling comfortable all the time.

By the same token, the best and biggest reward for C students is learning. Whenever you have the chance to acquire knowledge and skills relevant to your career goals, take the opportunity seriously. Though it may not seem like it at the time, learning is a much more significant reward early in your career than money, job perks, or prestige. I don't care what type of field you're in; the more you learn and grow, the more attention you'll receive. Executives notice the people who are hungry to learn. They admire those who ask questions, take on challenging tasks, and grow into their jobs.

As a C student who starts out without much of a reputation, your learning and growth are especially noticeable. People may not have high expectations of you at first, so when you exceed even those modest expectations, the company's leaders pay attention. This is why learning should be your most significant reward during the first ten years of your career. Most risks are worth taking if learning a key skill or acquiring critical experience are the rewards.

RISK AND FAILURE

Let's assume that you take a risk and it doesn't pay off. What happens? You fail. At the time this may seem like a career-destroying event. As a C student you assume this failure is going to be on your permanent record; that your screwup will follow you around from job to job. It's like receiving an F in algebra—when you first find out, it feels like your life is ruined.

Most job failures, though, don't leave a permanent mark. Unless you do something truly horrible like embezzle money or lose millions of dollars for your organization, you can bounce back from whatever mistake you made. For example, you may speak up during a meeting and your boss responds to your suggestion by saying, "That's a bad idea; you should know better." While you feel embarrassed in that moment and are convinced your boss will never trust you again, you'll have plenty of chances to redeem yourself. Though the risk of speaking up didn't pay off this time, the next time it might. People's memories are, thankfully, quite short when it comes to minor failures. They are also remarkably tolerant of an occasional failure. They will give you second, third, and fourth chances to succeed.

When I look back at my career, I can recall all types of failures. I have hired the wrong people, accepted clients I should have rejected, and made strategic blunders. If I would have taken these failures to heart, I probably would never have taken another major risk in these areas, and my career and the agency's business would have suffered. Instead, I kept taking the risks that had to be taken, and the majority of the time they paid off. I was able to take a step back from the failure, gain some perspective and realize that though it may have seemed like the end of the world at the time, it was really only a bump in the road.

I urge you to find the same perspective when you take a risk and it turns out badly. I would bet that every single person mentioned in this book has taken a risk that didn't pan out. Rich Melman has opened restaurants that didn't live up to expectations. Howie Carroll has probably backed political candidates who turned out to be losers. I know that Art Frigo has made at least one investment that he wishes he could take back. Nonetheless, I am certain that each one of these highly successful individuals learned a great lesson from whatever failures they experienced.

As painful as failure is, it is also necessary for success. Recall a bad grade you received in school. As much as it hurt to receive it, that grade probably also sent you a valuable message: You should study harder the next time; you don't have a future as a mathematician; or you should choose a topic that you really care about rather than one that seems easy.

The bottom line is to take risks, knowing that even if you fail you're likely to come out ahead. Always be smart about the risks you take, but also be smart about learning from any failures that come as a result.

CHAPTER 10

OVERCOME STRAIGHT-LINE THINKING

Many people think of careers as a straight line, a linear progression from one job to the next. They assume that with each job they will gain experience and expertise, preparing them for a better job the next time. They calculate that it will take x number of years to attain one career goal, y number of years to reach another goal.

C students should expect the unexpected. You might think to yourself that if you work hard you can obtain a management position by the time you're thirty or find employment at the top company in your field before you're thirty-five, but in reality your career will throw you some curves. If you're not prepared for these curves, you might have trouble dealing with them. In other words, when your plans don't work out, when you are fired, or when you end up hating the job you thought you'd love, you become distraught. Even worse, you become discouraged and may not think clearly about your next move. When your career goes off course, you beat yourself up for making mistakes and lose your drive. You may settle for a job you really don't want or become embittered and cynical.

In fact, you should expect to encounter roadblocks, curves, and other detours before achieving career goals. I did, and so did most of the people you've read about here. More often than not,

C students make a few false starts or fail in a job. They don't enter the job market as high potentials. But rather than become discouraged by setbacks and resigned to a less than ideal career path, they develop resiliency.

You have a choice. It's the same choice that I had when I was struggling at Heinz and in my first ad agency job. You can either become resigned to your "fate" or you can bounce back. Every single person you've read about has been confronted with this choice. From Art Frigo to Becky Jewett, all have faced events or circumstances that pushed them from the paths they were following. Instead of giving up or losing their drive, they drew energy from the obstacles they encountered. They went after their goals with renewed purpose and commitment.

To help you make the right choice when your career takes an unexpected turn, let's look at the types of detours you're likely to encounter and the right and wrong ways of responding.

FOUR TYPES OF UNEXPECTED TURNS

If you didn't take school seriously and if you haven't given much thought to what you want to do with your life, you may have to try a few different things before you find your true calling. Even if you did take school seriously and have a career plan in mind, you still may find it difficult to achieve it. Many people don't really know what they want to do until they are in the workforce for a while. It takes some real life experiences before you figure out what you should be doing.

Be aware that success is not always a straight line. More specifically, be prepared to encounter the following detours and dead ends in your career:

1. A PERIOD OF JOBLESSNESS.

It's doesn't seem like anyone will hire you for love or money. No matter how many job ads you respond to or interviews you go on, no one will make you an offer. While it's possible that you're doing something wrong—you come across poorly in interviews or you're applying for jobs for which you're unqualified—it's likely that you're the victim of bad luck or a bad job market. It's also possible that you're making a bad situation worse because you've developed a negative attitude.

Sometimes C students allow job turn-downs to become a self-fulfilling prophecy. They are convinced that they're not being hired because they are only average; that companies only hire A and B students. As a result they develop self-defeatist attitudes that come through in interviews or fail to apply for jobs because they're certain they don't stand a chance.

Persistence is the antidote to these attitudes. Refuse to give up or even slacken the pace of your job search. Remind yourself of the rules of probability: The more jobs you apply for, the more likely that one will come through. You should also tell yourself that there are few C students who haven't gone through the jobless doldrums, especially early in their careers. The way they emerged was by maintaining the intensity of their job search and their confidence in interviews. No matter how many rejections they had to endure, they continued to act as if their next interview would be the one that would result in an offer.

2. A BORING OR UNPLEASANT JOB.

Many of the people interviewed for this book talked about a job they hated or found boring. Mike Krasny knew he wasn't cut out to sell cars for his father's dealership. Art Frigo found working for 3M stifling. Norm Bobins might not have hated working in his family's business, but he knew it wasn't providing the challenges he wanted.

Sometimes you have to endure a bad job for a period of time because you need the money or the experience. If you're bored and not learning anything, ideally you'll find a new job as soon as possible. Still, everyone has to pay her dues, and if you're in a bad job, you should use it as a catalyst to think about the job you really want to have. What is it about this job that bores you? What specific tasks do you hate? What type of job will help you avoid these boring and hateful aspects?

More important, use these bad jobs as opportunities to envision what you'd like your ideal job to be. I hated stocking baby food in my first job for Heinz, but I had time to daydream about what I might do in the future. I remember picturing myself walking into meetings where I was in charge, of giving speeches, of making decisions that affected a lot of people. I wasn't clear on what specific job would allow me to do these things, but I had a clear idea of the types of responsibilities I wanted to have.

In other words, I used my down time to dream about what I might become. Too often, C students become so obsessed with what they hate about their bad jobs that they don't allow themselves to think beyond these jobs. Everyone needs a dream, or at least a vision of how their careers might evolve. You may have to adjust this vision at some point, but a vision provides something to shoot for and measure yourself against. I had a vision of myself as a leader, and I began to observe how others perceived me. Did I exhibit the qualities that people often associated with leadership? What leadership qualities did I lack that I needed to develop?

Dreaming helps make bad jobs tolerable, and it also provides C students with a road map toward a better future.

3. THE WRONG CAREER OR FIELD.

You realize that instead of being in sales, you should be in operations. Or you may discover that you really should be working for yourself rather than for someone else. Or that instead of being in business, you want to become an environmental lawyer. It's not unusual to find that your original career choice was the wrong one. While this usually happens relatively early in a career, it can also happen later on. Art Frigo had been working for a number of years before he launched his leveraged buyout and the beginning of his entrepreneurial career. Norm Bobins began working in the family business before he decided to go into banking. Becky Jewett had been employed for a number of years before she decided to go back to school for an MBA.

There is nothing wrong with any of this. What's wrong is sticking with something you know in your heart is wrong for you. You can make all sorts of excuses about why you're sticking with it—the money, you're too old to try something new, and so on—but as soon as you realize you're in the wrong place, you should at least start planning on making a change.

Remember, though, that you need to make a change in a positive direction. In other words, it's not enough to know that your job or field is wrong for you; you have to figure out what's right. It's great that you realize that being a banker isn't what you're passionate about, but you have to spend some time thinking about and exploring what you do care about. Make sure that you're not just reacting to an unpleasant job. Assess whether your commitment and energy might be renewed if you simply found another, better job in the same field.

Finally, accept that you might have to return to school to pursue your new field or accept a lower salary and start at the bottom if you make a career switch. These sacrifices, though, usually aren't that hard to make if you are pursuing your true calling and don't have major financial responsibilities.

4. GETTING FIRED.

This career detour can be especially devastating for C students. It is even worse than its aftermath—joblessness—since here you're being rejected by someone who knows you well. Getting fired isn't fun, but it also comes with the territory. You can't take it to heart. Companies go through tough economic times and have to downsize people regardless of their talent. People get fired because of personality conflicts with bosses. It does not mean that you're incompetent or have no future. It may mean that your personal style and talents are wrong for a given company. You may need to find a corporate culture that is more humanistic than your current one—or you may need one with more competitive challenges.

Take being fired as an opportunity for reflection and assessment. Some people fail to capitalize on this sort of opportunity, assuming that their boss is an idiot. Their analysis ends there. C students, on the other hand, reflexively think about what they did wrong to get themselves fired. They are used to questioning themselves rather than assuming the other person doesn't know what they're doing. Use this reflex. It may well be that the company made a big mistake in firing you and there's nothing to learn from the situation. On the other hand, you might learn a lot. Losing your job is jarring, and it makes you think about your career in ways you never would if things were going along smoothly.

For this reason, take advantage of being fired and reflect on the following:

- Why were you fired? Were you told that you lacked certain skills or knowledge that prevented you from doing your job effectively, or were you fired for reasons that had nothing to do with your competence?

- Do you believe that the company was the right place for you? Would you be happy to obtain a similar job in a similar type of company, or would you prefer to find a job in another type of company with a different culture? If so, what type of culture or position would you prefer?

- Is it possible that you belong in a different field or type of work setting? Did it seem as if you never fit in at your former company? Did you dream about a different type of job or work environment when you were employed there?

KEEP YOUR PERSPECTIVE AND DON'T PANIC

A new president was brought into a corporation Art Frigo was working for. Up until that point, Art was thriving as a member of the company, but this new boss made his life hell. At first, Art thought it was the worst thing that ever happened to him. But then he realized that "it was the best thing that ever happened to me. It taught me that I wasn't as in control of my career as I thought. It made me realize that I really wanted to be my own boss, and that's when I decided to launch a leveraged buyout of the company. I was reacting to a bad moment, and bad moments can catalyze your career; they can wake you up."

When we find ourselves in similar situations we view them as crises and often jump to the wrong conclusions and take misguided actions. For instance, you may believe that being stuck in a boring job means there must be something wrong with you and you should try to stick it out and learn to like it. Or you may be without a job for weeks and months and conclude that you'll never get a job or that you should take the first position that's offered, whether or not it seems right for you.

Most people blow negative events out of proportion. A bad performance review will seem like the end of the world to some. Others wake up in the middle of the night and realize that they have been in the wrong field for the past three years, feeling like they've made a fatal mistake. Even now, I occasionally overreact to negative events—the loss of a client or a key person leaving the agency—and initially believe it's going to cause big problems. In most instances, though, my experience helps me put these events in perspective and I understand that in a day or two the crisis will have passed. I don't mean to minimize these events or suggest that it's easy to replace either clients or people. My point is that it helps to remain calm so that you don't make hasty or unwise decisions.

Having a boss or mentor you can talk to helps a lot to put a crisis into context. Many times his experience and wisdom can help you see the crisis for what it is rather than what your fears turn it into. Al Eicoff served this role for me. Rich Melman had a partner a few years older than him when he started out who functioned in a similar manner. Senator Howard Carroll was able to turn to Mayor Daley.

Even if you don't have a mentor or a boss whom you feel comfortable discussing these issues with, look for an old pro in your organization or outside of it who might help you put a crisis in perspective. Perhaps you developed a relationship with a headhunter who will lend a sympathetic ear when you're facing a crisis. It's possible that someone in your company's human resources department can help you. The key is not to keep all your fears bottled up inside. When you aren't able to talk with someone who has been where you are, the issues can become magnified in your mind. Sharing your fears and hearing how other people responded in similar circumstances will often enable you to look at these situations with greater logic and objectivity.

SIGNS OF PROGRESS

People often judge their career success or failure based on salary, job title, and type of employer. These are significant measurements, but they should not be the only ones you use. You may be making great strides in terms of acquiring knowledge, learning new skills, developing valuable relationships, or changing people's perceptions of your abilities, and none of these things may register as progress in your mind. If you persist in these efforts, though, eventually they will translate into tangible success. Regularly measuring your progress in this respect provides motivation to succeed in other areas rather than pursuing more money or more prestigious job titles exclusively.

Keeping a journal is a good way to chart your progress. Whenever you acquire a new skill or piece of knowledge, enter it in the journal. You don't have to note every minor learning that takes place, but you should recognize significant achievements. For instance, if you're in sales and you finally figured out how to use your company's system for capturing leads and mining the customer database, that is worthy of mention. Similarly, if you feel you're becoming a more effective leader—if you find that you're able to take leading roles in teams and that other people look to you for guidance—that, too, is an entry worth making.

You should also chart your relationships and whether you're establishing a strong network within and outside of your organization. Recognize when you've made a contact with someone higher up in the organization who seems to enjoy talking with and helping you. Note when you have established a relationship with someone who is willing to assist you in achieving goals. Identify people of influence who have become part of your network. Establishing, expanding, and strengthening these relationships represents real progress.

Besides entering these achievements in a journal, pay attention to any changes in how you're perceived within an organization. In many ways this is the most significant indication of progress, and positive changes often signal that promotions, raises, and other perks are on their way. For instance, assess whether people perceive you as the prototypical C student. Do they see you as average because of the school you went to, the way you dress, how you conduct yourself in meetings and interactions with higher-level people? You may have already typecast yourself, but while you can't change the facts, you can change the behaviors—and other people's perceptions. Though I went to the University of Arizona, I would proclaim, "Yes, I went to the University of Arizona, the Harvard of the West." Just because you are viewed as a C student initially doesn't mean you can't change some or all of the negative connotations of that assessment.

Some bosses have only modest expectations for C students. They may view them as good people with decent abilities but lacking the drive or skills necessary for outstanding achievement. Over time, though, as you have a chance to demonstrate what you can do, this perception may change. You can see the change in a million small ways: people show you more respect, your boss gives you more challenging assignments, you are placed on teams composed primarily of people who have more experience than you possess, people start asking you for information and advice, and so on. When they start treating you in ways that are different from when you first joined the organization, that is a clear sign of progress.

When I joined Eicoff, people had no idea what my role was and how I was adding value to the agency. Their perception of me was not positive. To some employees, I was a young, aggressive guy in over his head whom the agency president had taken a liking to. After I had been at the agency for a little less than a year, Al Eicoff asked me to go to Canada with Marge Zolla, one of the agency's media buyers, to help a relatively new account get off the ground. But at the meeting, the head of the company, an imposing man named Mr. Black, tore into us for our alleged shortcomings. I responded by addressing each of his points and promising to resolve each issue he raised. It wasn't so much what I said as how I said it. I was always good at thinking on my feet and communicating my commitment to my clients. By the end of the meeting, Mr. Black's mood had brightened considerably. In fact, he seemed like a different person, our friend rather than our enemy. When we walked out of the meeting, Marge turned to me and said, "Now I know what you do." When we returned to the agency, Marge told everyone what had transpired and perceptions changed almost immediately.

People often recall major events, such as receiving a big promotion or achieving some financial goal, as the turning points in their careers. My turning point was this change in perception. From that moment on I was given the respect and support I needed to succeed.

JEALOUSY IS THE ENEMY

It is very easy to succumb to jealousy when you're starting out. You see A students securing top jobs with big companies as lawyers, consultants, bankers, and stockbrokers, and you think that you're always going to be behind. You envy their early success and feel as if you have to play catch-up. For this reason, you pay more attention to what a job pays than whether you're energized by it.

You concentrate more on your title than whether you're learning and growing. In short, your envy causes you to make bad career decisions.

Here is a cautionary tale that may help you think twice before you succumb to envy. I had been at Eicoff for a few years when a client invited me to his house to play tennis. This client, let's call him Dan, was an extremely wealthy businessman, and when I drove up to his mansion in an affluent Chicago suburb, I saw some examples of how he was spending his money. The house was one of the largest and most ornate that I had ever seen—and he had also built a tennis court, a swimming pool, and hockey rink on the grounds. When I rang the doorbell, Dan's wife answered, and she of course was beautiful. Dan and I played singles and then were joined by two of Dan's friends for doubles. One of the friends pulled up to the house in a top-of-the-line Mercedes, and it turned out he was an advertising legend—let's call him Tim. After we played tennis, we talked for a while; I was tremendously impressed by Tim. He carried himself with class, was incredibly bright, and had achieved both fame and fortune at a relatively young age.

When I drove away from the house, I thought to myself that both Dan and Tim had it made. For the first time in my life, I envied someone else's success.

Fast forward five or so years: Dan blew his entire fortune as a result of drug use, and Tim was in jail after committing a crime that tarnished his reputation.

The lesson: Don't envy others, because you might not be so envious if you knew the full story. The next time you feel yourself becoming jealous of a colleague, someone you went to school with or a customer or client, remind yourself that all you're envying is the surface of their success. While it's possible that these individuals are happy, ethical, and fulfilled human beings, it's just as possible that they are unhappy, unethical, and unfulfilled. Envy will get you nowhere except closer to being embittered.

A much more productive way of looking at other people's success is as a learner. What have they done that is worth emulating? Do they have a particular style of leadership or management that you can learn from? Is their success a result of hard work, gumption, taking risks, persistence, creativity? When did they display these qualities and under what circumstances? Are there certain actions they took that you should consider?

By the same token, did these successful individuals make sacrifices or take chances that you're unwilling to make or take? Don't try to copy another person's path to success. Don't let your envy blind you to specific behavior that feels wrong to you.

KEEP THE NINE GUIDELINES IN MIND

Some of the suggestions found in this book will be easier to follow than others, so don't feel you have to do everything. Some C students can succeed without a mentor; others can achieve their goals even if they don't take smart risks. The preceding chapters have each offered specific guidelines, recognizing that you're going to have to figure out which ones work best for you. Some of you may be five or ten years into your careers and have already found a mentor, so you may be more interested in other suggestions, such as becoming a purposeful learner. If you're a recent college graduate, on the other hand, finding a mentor may strike you as a logical first step.

However you decide to proceed, the following checklists will make it easier to implement each of the nine guidelines.

1. MAKE THE MOST OUT OF MANY MENTORS.

- Keep your mind open and don't rule people out because they don't seem to fit a narrow definition of what a mentor should be.

- Pay attention to people who pay attention to you, who are interested in telling you stories and sharing information.

- Let the relationship develop naturally. Don't force yourself on someone; get to know a prospective mentor and let her know you.

- Don't stop looking because you don't find a mentor immediately. Don't develop a C student's inferiority complex and feel that no one would be interested in adopting you.

- Don't limit yourself to one mentor. You can draw on different people for different types of help.

2. TRUST YOUR INSTINCT.

- Every month, take a step back to determine whether all your decisions and actions were made based on logic or if you occasionally acted purely on instinct.

- If you have trouble acting on instinct, practice doing so when the outcomes aren't particularly significant.

- Think about how you've trusted your gut successfully in areas outside of work; how it has helped you find your spouse, make good investments, choose friends, and so on.

- Be sure to listen to what that voice inside your head tells you when you're facing tough decisions such as whether to accept a new job, how to resolve a complex problem at work, and so on.

3. STRIVE TO BE A BETTER PERSON THAN AN EMPLOYEE.

- Make a consistent effort to listen to colleagues who have problems, help people who are struggling, and respect your coworkers, customers, and suppliers.

- Do not fool yourself into thinking that you can have one set of values for your personal life and another set for work.

- Repeat to yourself that nice guys finish first; that though some not-so-nice people do succeed through talent or game-playing, they are the exceptions rather than the rule.

4. TAKE RESPONSIBILITY SERIOUSLY.

- Adopt a volunteer mentality and raise your hand when your boss or others in your company request help.

- Take pride in whatever job you're doing, even if it might seem inconsequential or you don't particularly like doing it.

- As tempted as you are to make excuses or find scapegoats when a project you're responsible for goes awry, resist this temptation. Resist even when there are legitimate excuses or someone else messed up.

- Do more than others expect—complete projects before deadlines, conduct additional research, and offer ideas and conclusions that require thought and analysis that go beyond the norm.

5. MASTER THE ART OF PURPOSEFUL LEARNING.

- Be especially alert for opportunities to learn from failures. Don't react defensively and tune out negative data, but make an effort to learn from failures so you don't make the same mistake twice.

- Treat your first few jobs after college as a type of graduate school. Focus on building your knowledge and skills as much if not more than excelling in your job. Use this learning to make yourself into a marketable commodity.

- Make an effort to acquire tacit knowledge—the unspoken truths about how work gets done, red tape is circumvented, scarce resources are found, and so on.

- Set long-term goals for short-term learning. Consider the ideal job you hope to have down the road, figure out the knowledge and skills this job requires, and start concentrating on obtaining them.

6. TAKE ADVANTAGE OF UNEXPECTED OPPORTUNITIES.

- Watch for opportunities that fly under the radar. Evaluate jobs based on whether they provide strong learning environments, give you the chance to develop skills that you might not get elsewhere, offer you challenges that you might not face for years at other companies.

- Pay special attention to opportunities that help you develop your creativity, become better at execution, and give you the chance to become a more effective leader.

- Don't rule out opportunities simply because they pay less than you would like or require you to work for a smaller, less-well-known company than you would prefer.

7. SELL WHAT YOU BELIEVE.

- Recognize that whether or not your job involves formal sell-ing, developing your ability to sell will give you an advantage over others who may have a better education or better connec-tions than you possess.

- Sell honestly, not cynically. When you try to convince some-one of something, be sure you've convinced yourself first—do not sell products, services, policies, or programs you have seri-ous reservations about.

- Develop a selling style based on your personality. Use humor, be direct, employ charm, or rely on networking as befits who you are.

- Practice selling regularly. Hone the techniques that work for you and make a consistent effort with colleagues, subordi-nates, bosses, customers, vendors, and others to present your point of view convincingly.

8. GO WHERE THE STARS AREN'T.

- Be innovative about the types of jobs you apply for. Consider a wide range of employment possibilities, and translate what-ever unique strengths or knowledge you possess into job assets during employment interviews.

- Look for companies that have a significant need for your par-ticular skills and talents. Search for organizations where you won't be one of many similarly skilled people fighting for one job, but where you offer something different than others.

- Resolve not to overstay your welcome. Pay attention to your feelings of boredom or when you feel unchallenged for a sustained period of time. Accept that you're never going to be a star as long as you're just going through the motions.

9. BE A SMART RISK-TAKER.

- Be aware that C students must take at least some risks to achieve significant rewards. If you play it safe and never speak up or try something new, you will be giving up a major way to gain recognition and respect.

- Determine whether you're a low, medium, or high risk taker. Take risks in accordance with your profile.

- Test your capacity for risk by starting out at the low end of the continuum. Ask for help and express a different opinion to begin, and then move on to more difficult types of risks once you feel comfortable taking low-end ones.

- Resolve not to let fear of failure prevent you from taking any risks. Accept that some risks taken will result in failure, and while these are not pleasant experiences, they can help you learn and grow.

Keep this checklist handy, especially when you encounter setbacks and are confused about your next career steps. Odds are, at least one of these nine guidelines will give you some constructive advice and diminish your confusion about what to do next.

RESOURCES: PREPARING FOR A ZIGZAG ROAD TO THE TOP

Just as you wouldn't begin a long journey without adequate supplies, you shouldn't embark on a career without resources. Specifically, you should build a reserve of people, knowledge, and money that will come in handy when you hit an inevitable career obstacle. Anyone can accumulate these resources, regardless of age, experience, or expertise. Surprisingly, though, many people don't do so. Some people are so arrogant that they believe they can handle anything on their own, and they don't have to prepare in any way for their careers. So when they're blindsided by a negative career event such as being fired, they have no idea which way to turn. They flounder because they have not prepared themselves for unexpected developments and setbacks.

The following are three types of resources you should gather as you move forward in your career:

1. PEOPLE.

You don't have to go it alone. As a C student, you're in the majority. There are plenty of other people in your field who have gone through or are going through the same things, and they will be willing to help you. This help can take many forms, from providing a sympathetic ear to telling you about job openings. I was a member of the Young Presidents' Organization (YPO), as were some of the other individuals discussed in the book. It was great to be able to talk honestly and openly with other relatively young CEOs who were in similar situations. Over the years YPO has been a source of both intellectual and emotional support, and I knew I could count on YPO members when I found myself facing roadblocks.

I realize that most of you aren't presidents of your organizations yet and YPO isn't available to you. Until you reach that point, though, you have access to many different groups, from industry associations to young professional clubs based in your city. Many of these groups offer seminars and workshops as well as less formal opportunities to meet and talk with peers.

You should also make an effort to establish relationships with a diverse group of people within your workplace and maintain these relationships even after you or they leave the company. I'm not just talking about socializing with coworkers but exchanging information and ideas, talking about career aspirations, and offering help when help is needed.

Both in the short and long term, the people you know will prove to be an invaluable resource. It you're skilled at establishing relationships and diligent about maintaining them, within a few years you can build a network that you can turn to in good times and bad. Remember, you don't have the luxury of being a rugged individualist. Your career is not going to be based on your sterling credentials or family connections. It is going to be built on relationships, and these relationships are especially crucial when you find yourself struggling because you're having trouble meeting your performance objectives, are downsized out of a job, or are confused about your next career move.

2. KNOWLEDGE.

I've talked about the importance of purposeful learning, but knowledge can also serve as a resource when you face problems or have questions about your career. You never know what piece of information or new idea will be useful, so it makes sense to acquire a broad base of knowledge. Certainly this last statement applies to your job and industry, but it also applies to knowledge in general. I read a lot—not just books about business, but about history and politics, for example. I take a great interest in the world around me, and I listen closely to what people have to say, especially when they are talking about their areas of expertise. You never know when a stray fact or idea can create a connection with a client or when something you read about in a book can be translated into business strategy.

In today's information age, the Internet makes an overwhelming amount of data immediately accessible. Take advantage of the technology. There will come a time when everyone is stumped by a problem during a meeting. If you're more knowledgeable than the other people at the meeting, you're more likely to come up with a solution. Knowledge might also help you better chart your career direction, giving you insights into the advantages of either going into a specific type of business or joining a start-up company.

The more successful people I know also are the most knowledgeable. This isn't coincidence. By knowledgable, I don't mean the smartest. Instead, they know their jobs and their fields better than anyone else. I defy you to find anyone who is more politically astute than Howard Carroll or savvier about restaurants than Rich Melman or better informed about the gaming industry than Dino Child. They have made it a point to know their business better than their competitors. They spend a lot of time reading and listening to news about their industries, but they also invest a lot of thinking time, spotting emerging industry trends and analyzing how they might unfold. As a result, they are prepared in good times and bad, and they are able to respond faster and more effectively because they've considered all their options in advance.

3. MONEY.

You look at the world differently when you have money in the bank. Of course, when you're starting out, you haven't had the time or the type of jobs to accumulate much money, but a little in reserve can have a dramatic impact on how you approach your job and your career. If you're living from paycheck to paycheck, you're naturally going to be fearful of losing your job or jeopardizing it in any way. You'll be reluctant to speak your mind or take a risk.

If you can build a bit of a financial cushion for yourself, on the other hand, you can take more risks and gain a measure of independence. You don't need a huge amount—just enough to live on for six months or a year if you were to find yourself jobless. With this money in the bank, you will be much more likely to challenge the conventional wisdom and assert yourself. Most organizations are looking for independent-minded, assertive people, and you can emerge as one if you're not terrified of being fired for being too assertive. A small financial cushion also makes it easier to make a break from a job you should leave. If you're bored and unchallenged, you can actively search for a new position or even leave the old one, knowing you can get by for a period of time.

AMBITION AND PATIENCE: THE PARADOX OF GETTING AHEAD

Never forget that your career, like Rome, isn't built in a day. Art Frigo worked for a number of companies before he became an entrepreneur. Norm Bobins worked in his family's business and then for American National Bank before he joined Exchange National Bank and his career took off. They all exhibited a degree of patience, biding their time by learning and growing and preparing themselves for the opportunity that they instinctively knew would come along.

At the same time, they were ambitious. They dreamed big and were aggressive in pursuing their dreams. To varying degrees they pushed hard to achieve their career goals.

The paradox is that they were simultaneously ambitious and patient. As hard as they pushed, they didn't become greedy and ruthless. They recognized that ambition must have limits or it can become self-destructive. None of the high achievers I've profiled has the capacity to be Enron's Jeff Skilling. They managed the paradox of ambition and patience by tempering the former with the latter, especially during the first five or ten years of their careers. When they encountered obstacles, they didn't blindly rush forward or steamroll anyone in their way. In most instances, they patiently waited until the time was right to act, maintaining their integrity as they moved toward their goals.

This is my final piece of advice to you. As a C student, there are times when you're not going to be moving in a straight line toward your goals, and this is going to be frustrating. I would counsel patience in these instances. When you've been fired from a job or find yourself feeling stuck in your career, take some time to reflect on your options. Get out of the office and go for a walk. Find a place where you can get some perspective on your situation. Ask yourself if you're guilty of having unrealistic expectations of a job or yourself at this point in your career. Determine whether your frustration is temporary and caused by a single incident or if it's long lasting and a result of the environment in which you work. Only then can you determine if your ambitions can be fulfilled where you are or if you need to take alternative actions.

Never forget that C students can achieve great things. I've discussed only a relatively small number of people here, people who started with some type of handicap and became amazingly successful CEOs, entrepreneurs, lawyers, bankers, and restaurateurs. If you look around, you'll find C students, late starters, and others who were not initially on the fast track but who became leaders in their fields. My most sincere hope is that the stories and advice I've shared here will inspire you to join their ranks.

ACKNOWLEDGMENTS

First and foremost, I would like to thank all the people I interviewed for this book. Everyone provided great insights and stories; I learned from the former and was inspired by the latter. Some of you are longtime friends and others I met for the first time in our interviews, but I'm honored that all of you shared your experiences for publication.

I also would like to acknowledge the contributions of the entire Eicoff agency, especially Bonnie Brunsell, for coordinating the many details involved in putting this book together; the late Alvin Eicoff, for being exactly the right mentor and for being a pioneering genius in our industry; and Shelly Lazarus, Ogilvy Worldwide (Eicoff's parent company) president and CEO, for teaching me lessons about business that aren't found in books.

I also am tremendously appreciative of Eicoff clients past and present for not only helping me to understand your business but the value of relationships.

Thanks also to my friend Bruce Wexler, whose editorial skills and book-publishing savvy helped make this book a reality.

I am also appreciative of the work done by my agent, Daniel Greenberg, who found the ideal publisher for this project. And speaking of that publisher, I would like to thank my editor, Mitch Horowitz, and everyone at Tarcher for recognizing that C students need a book like this and helping to make it the best book it could possibly be.

Finally, I would be remiss if I didn't thank my daughter, Debbie, my son, Michael, and my wife, Linda, for their support and love; I could not have written this book without both.

Norm Bobins

Norm started his career by working in his family's business, a small manufacturing operation run by Norm's father and his uncle. They encouraged Norm, who already had his MBA, to take a few years off from the business and gain experience elsewhere. They assumed this experience would prove valuable and help him when he eventually returned and later on when he took over the family business. They suggested banking would be a good area in which to gain experience, and Norm got a job with American National Bank. He flourished in the banking environment and found that, unlike many of his more conservative colleagues, he was able to trust his instinct in lending situations. His instinct combined with his analytical abilities helped him rise to be one of the top fifteen officers in the then $2 billion bank.

Norm had been at American for fourteen years in 1981, when an opportunity arose at Exchange National Bank, and he accepted the position, even though Exchange was significantly smaller than American. Norm recognized he was taking a risk, but his instincts told him it was a good risk to take. He turned out to be right, since exchange eventually combined with LaSalle National Bank to form what is now a $110 billion bank. Norm was elected president and then chairman, the position he holds today.

Dennis Bookshester

CEO of retailing giants Carson Pirie Scott, Zales Jewelry, and Fruit of the Loom, Dennis started his career as a shoe salesman. Dennis's father died when Dennis was seventeen, and he had to work to support his family. Instead of taking pre-med courses in college, he began working in department stores. Even without the benefit of an MBA from a top school, Dennis was quickly deemed to have executive potential and was placed in a training program. He became the CEO of a $200 million company when he was only thirty-seven.

Dennis's father had had a small retail business, so Dennis grew up recognizing the importance of numbers and the need to "make his numbers." Even though he moved up through the ranks in a marketing and merchandising track, he was smart about finances and he always made sure he had a top financial person working with him. He also took pride in creating environments where people felt comfortable sharing both bad news and good news. Brilliant at delegating to people who "knew more than he did," he would take great pride in accepting responsibility for the success or failure of projects he was in charge of. His ability to attract top talent and maximize other people's potential made him a great leader early in his career, and it led to a series of high-profile CEO positions where no one cared that he had started out as a shoe salesman.

Howard Carroll

Howie (as he is affectionately known to his friends) served in the Illinois legislature for twenty-eight years, was the 50th Ward Democratic Committeeman for twenty years, and was considered the number two person in the party hierarchy during this time. Just as significantly, Howie also was well known for his kindness, devotion to good causes, and ability to resolve conflicts. A protégé

of the late Chicago mayor Richard J. Daley and law school class-
mate of the current mayor, Richard M. Daley, Howie demonstrated an uncanny ability to survive and prosper in the highly
competitive world of Chicago politics.

Though Howie didn't attend one of the country's top
law schools or look like a Kennedy, he parlayed his affability,
relationship-building skills, and sharp political instincts into an
enormously successful career. For years he was the go-to guy in the
Illinois senate and gained tremendous respect for his knowledge
about financial issues. In a field where connections count, Howie
knew everyone worth knowing.

Today, Howie is a highly respected Chicago attorney.

Dino Child

Dino dropped out of college to make a career of the gaming industry in Las Vegas, and it was a gamble that paid off, leading to
the position of director of player development at the Venetian.
Though he was just an okay student, he was a natural in the gaming industry. He worked his way up from the bottom, starting as a
busboy and server in Vegas restaurants, moving on to the casino
floor and working as a dealer and then a pit boss, and finally making it into the management ranks.

Along the way, Dino demonstrated that he took responsibility
seriously, impressing his bosses. More than that, he brought a passion and energy to his work that resulted in a series of promotions. He was also terrific at learning exactly what he needed to
know to do well at each new position, and being a quick study
helped him excel faster than others. The gaming industry is a
tough, highly competitive business, but Dino has succeeded at it
not by being a cutthroat competitor but by doing his job extremely well and being a decent person to boot.

Richard Donchin

Richard is the president of the Elston Ace Hardware Company, a chain of six Chicago-area stores. His father originally owned one hardware store, and Richard helped expand the business by taking a series of well-calculated risks. Like many C students, he was willing to take risks that others weren't, and consequently became one of the most successful Ace retailers in the country.

Richard never graduated from college, but he made it his business to know the hardware business better than anyone. When he talks about what has made him successful, it always goes back to being a purposeful learner. Competitors may have more financial resources and more MBAs, but no one understands hardware store customers and their requirements better than Richard. He also has built an esprit de corps among his employees, and in a business where people tend to move around frequently, he has maintained remarkable employee loyalty.

Craig Duchossois

Craig holds a BBA and MBA from Southern Methodist University and currently is CEO of Duchossois Industries, a company with interests in transportation, consumer and defense products, entertainment, and venture capital. He also serves on the boards of LaSalle National Bank, Trinity Industries, Churchill Downs, the University of Chicago, Culver Educational Foundation, and the Illinois Institute of Technology. He was also an officer in the U.S. Marine Corps from 1968 to 1971.

When Craig joined the family business, his challenge was to make a name for himself in relation to his highly accomplished father, Richard. Craig's dad not only founded Duchossois Industries but achieved a high profile by purchasing the Arlington Park Racetrack from Madison Square Garden Corporation in 1983 and turning it into one of the country's premier thoroughbred racing facilities. Craig is now CEO of Duchossois Industries, a privately held diversified operating company with interests in access control, advanced control, and automation; venture capital; and entertainment.

Flip Filipowski

A product of military school who never finished college, Flip started as a computer operator at Time, Inc., then joined Motorola, went to AB Dick, and finally landed at software giant Cullinet in 1973 as COO. In 1987, he started software pioneer Platinum Technologies, growing it to the eighth largest software enterprise in the world (at the time) and sold it in 1999 for $4 billion. Flip received many honors during these years, including being named by *Upside* magazine as one of the top 100 most influential people in information technology. He also launched Divine Inc., a visionary company that was designed as an "Internet zaibatsu," essentially a synergistic collection of high-tech companies. In the process Flip hoped to place Chicago on a par with Silicon Valley and other high-tech centers. It was a grand vision that ultimately didn't work out, but it exemplified the risk-taking, visionary approach to business that made Flip's grades in school irrelevant to his success.

Flip's success was predicated on taking risks, operating on instinct, finding unexpected opportunities, and many of the other qualities of highly successful C students. He has recently launched SilkRoad Technologies, and no doubt he will have another winner with this and other future ventures.

Art Frigo

Art had a number of false starts early in his career before he found his true calling as an entrepreneur. When he worked in sales for 3M, he sensed he was not in the right place, despite his success there. After going back to school to further his education and working for a consulting firm, Art orchestrated one of the first leveraged buyouts in U.S. history and started his entrepreneurial career.

Over the years, Art has successfully started and grown companies in diverse fields, including auto racing, food, and cleaning products. In this last group, he was CEO of M.B. Walton, makers of the Roll-O-Matic Mop and other related products. Art, a former adjunct professor at Northwestern University's Kellogg School of Management, is currently the chairperson of Kellogg's Larry and Carol Levy Entrepreneurial Institute and is a frequent lecturer at the school.

Besides being an incredibly sharp businessperson, Art has an infectiously upbeat attitude and a great ability to mentor others.

Becky Jewett

At first glance, Becky may seem to be as far from a C student as you can get. She went to college at Wellesley and earned her MBA at Harvard. Yet despite this educational pedigree, she encountered similar career roadblocks and problems that C students face when she was starting out. Back in the 1970s, Becky found that being a woman was a handicap if you aspired to be in management, at least in certain companies. She even had to learn to type in order to get a job. Fortunately, she found a mentor who helped her obtain her first management job. Her career stalled, though, because she only had her degree from Wellesley at this point, so she enrolled in Harvard to gain credibility.

With her MBA in hand, she pursued a career in direct marketing, moving from one clothing direct marketer to the next in positions of increasing responsibility, eventually becoming president of Chadwick's. Though most top direct-marketing executives back then were men, Becky's street smarts (along with her academic smarts) stood her in good stead, and she impressed everyone with her grasp of direct-selling principles. A former chairperson of the Direct Marketing Association's board and past president of Norm Thompson outfitters, Becky has more than leveled the playing field through her intelligence and determination.

Mike Krasny

Founder and chairman emeritus of CDW Inc. (formerly known as Computer Discount Warehouse), Mike built the company, a direct seller of computer products, into a $5 billion company. An indifferent student (except for computer science), Mike began his career as a used-car salesman at his family's dealership. His "education," though, involved spending a lot of time in computer stores, and it was there that he came up with his idea for an alternative sales model: buying and reselling computers.

Mike started his business by taking out an ad in the *Chicago Tribune* classified section. The rest is history. His business grew by leaps and bounds until he had thousands of employees and Mike was named 1993 Entrepreneur of the Year by *Inc.* and *Financial World* magazines. During his stewardship, Mike displayed the sort of take-charge, involved attitude that is rare among CEOs. He would work alongside his employees to make sure shipments got out on time, and displayed a passion for his work and compassion for his employees that helped CDW become so successful.

Larry Levy

Though Larry was an excellent student with an MBA from Northwestern University, he did not take the traditional route of most of his classmates. Rather than aspire to work for a corporation, Larry wanted to be an entrepreneur, a career that at the time (1967) was viewed by many of his peers and professors as less desirable than a corporate career. When he and his brother opened a delicatessen in Chicago, they struggled initially. Their passion for food and their ingenuity, however, eventually turned the restaurant into a success.

In the ensuing years, Larry expanded his operation in pioneering directions. Taking risks, using his instinct, and drawing investors to him because of his business sense and honesty, Larry created a new category of foodservice enterprise, one that provides upscale catering for professional athletic events (football, basketball, and baseball stadiums) and entertainment forums including the Grammy Awards.

Rich Melman

As founder and chairman of Lettuce Entertain You Enterprises (LEYE), Rich is arguably the most successful nonchain restaurateur in the country. The company owns and manages more than sixty-five restaurants, including Wildfire and Ambria.

Like many of the people described in the book, Rich was not a stellar student, but he did well at things he was passionate about, such as sports. Food, though, was his first love, and he demonstrated an ability to take risks by opening innovative restaurants and trusting his instincts that these risks would pay off. He built LEYE with more than just his instincts and risk-taking ability, though. He created a company that emphasized straight talk and honest, caring relationships, which produced a culture that has helped the company succeed and grow in an industry where relatively few restaurant companies prosper for long.

Sam Morasca

A Penn State graduate and a Boston College MBA who worked for Shell Oil all of his career, Sam picked Shell over other companies because he recognized they were not going to treat him like one of the masses. Even though he didn't go to one of the highly elite MBA programs, Sam saw that Shell would judge him on his merits, which is all a typical student could ask for. Still, he was not initially on the fast track. But he placed himself on it over time by taking responsibility seriously. Sam volunteered for one project after the next, and he did more with these projects than most people would. Surpassing his bosses' expectations with each assignment and position, Shell management gradually realized they had someone special.

As a result of this recognition and Sam's character and team skill, he began receiving one promotion after the next. Sam also had the handicap of not being an engineer in a company whose management ranks were filled with engineers and others with technical backgrounds. Time and again, he overcome this handicap and ended his career at Shell as the top sales and marketing executive.

Louise O'Sullivan

Now the founder and president of Prime Advantage, a manufacturer's buying group with over $17 billion in purchasing power, Louise started this new and highly successful phase of her career at age fifty-one! Louise spent the previous twenty-two years working for Groen, a manufacturer of commercial foodservice and industrial processing equipment, eventually becoming the company's president. This simple fact is remarkable for two reasons. First, Louise started her career as an elementary school teacher, and she joined Groen part-time as a technical writer. Second, Groen was a male-dominated business where women were viewed primarily as clerical or support staff.

Louise, however, used her aggressiveness, instinct, and communication skills to seize every opportunity that came her way. She quickly became recognized for her marketing and sales abilities and was promoted far beyond where any woman had gone at Groen before her. Besides receiving many honors during her career at Groen, her successful tenure there became a Harvard Business School case study.

Mike Waters

Mike describes himself as having suffered from attention deficit disorder as a boy, getting poor grades, and not taking school seriously. Though he didn't do well in school, he demonstrated great mechanical aptitude from an early age, and this ability to "take things apart and put them back together" guided him in his choice of careers. At first, though, he ignored this talent, not even taking an engineering course in college. For a number of years he worked for his father's company and was involved in everything but product design.

It was only when circumstances forced him to use his engineering skills that he started designing products. Soon after, he started building companies around the products he designed. He discovered that he had a talent not only for creating highly marketable products but for selling them with great commitment and energy. A number of those products, including LitterMaid, have been enormously successful, and Waters Industries has flourished ever since.

INDEX

ABOUT THE AUTHOR

An average student, Ron Bliwas is currently President/CEO of A. Eicoff & Co., a Chicago-based advertising agency that is a division of Ogilvy & Mather. Ron is married, has two children, and lives in the Chicago area.